1986

BASIC ISSUES IN MASS COMMUNICATION

Basic Issues in MASS COMMUNICATION

A Debate

Everette E. Dennis *University of Oregon*

John C. Merrill *Louisiana State University*

Macmillan Publishing Company
New York

Collier Macmillan Publishers
London

Macmillan Publishing Co., Inc.
866 Third Avenue, New York, New York 10022

Collier Macmillan Canada, Inc.

Library of Congress Cataloging in Publication Data

Dennis, Everette E.
  Basic issues in mass communication.

  Includes index.
  1. Mass media—United States. I. Merrill, John
Calhoun, 1924–   . II. Title.
P92.U5D44   1984   001.51'0973   83-1021
ISBN 0-02-328510-9

Printing: 1 2 3 4 5 6 7 8   Year: 4 5 6 7 8 9 0 1

ISBN   0-02-328510-9

Preface

At first glance it may appear that many contemporary issues in journalism and mass communication are trendy, faddish, and ephemeral. What is vital and compelling today may seem dated or passé tomorrow. A television network sues the government; a reporter goes to jail for refusing to divulge sources; a critic calls the press unprofessional; minorities say they are not represented in the media; a newspaper dies; the President says the press is too powerful. These topical issues are more than a passing show. They are part of continuing controversies, of enduring issues that have molded our communications system in the United States.

This book examines some of these persistent arguments that puzzle and perplex editors, broadcasters, critics, educators, and others who are concerned about the purposes and practices of the mass media in America. We have selected thirteen of the most common and recurring themes in debates about journalism, the media, and the press. In most instances a lively, contemporary controversy can be examined in the context of a conventional tenet or "article of faith" about the media in America. It is not uncommon for antagonisms to flare up over whether the prevailing mode of thought about the issue is adequate or needs to be reconsidered or replaced. We have tried to recreate that spirit in this book.

First, we selected the issues; then we phrased them in an adversarial style and argued our positions by assembling evidence. The format of this book is a departure from standard journalism texts. Each of the thirteen issues is succinctly defined and explained. The prevailing sentiment on each of them is identified. Then, one of us challenges the contemporary view while the other offers a response. We do this to identify the central questions at the core of the debate and to demonstrate how and why people quite legitimately have such different views. In this adversarial manner, we reduce a number of complex subjects to stark pro and con arguments. We do this because this is the way they are most often raised by others, but we also point up the many complexities that ought to be considered before anyone comes to a reasoned conclusion. Still, issues like these typically are resolved through compromise. Such decisions require choices that relate evidence, values, and practical solutions to problems.

We hope that readers of this book, whether students or media professionals, will find that it stimulates their thinking as they confront these continuing issues that have plagued, perplexed, and excited others over the years. The subjects presented here are organized in such a way that they help the reader explore the nature, purpose, and operations of mass communication in America. Some of the issues raised are writ large with social implications while others border on internal "shop talk." However, taken together they help us understand the relationship of the communications media to society as well as the relationship of social forces to the press and mass communication.

In selecting the issues presented here, we perused scores of books, articles, bibliographies, and other scholarly inventories to assure ourselves that we were choosing both the most prevalent and most important arguments for analysis here. The thirteen issues singled out are developed with more than one hundred subsidiary issues.

Whenever possible, we point up the links between and among the various professional and scholarly controversies considered here, explaining how and why they are interrelated. For example, we begin with a debate that defines and explores freedom of the press. This is tied to a resolution of the proper relationship between media and government. Then, we look at two recurring themes with regard to "press rights" and people's rights, the matters of the "right to know" and "public access to the media." These and other issues are not mere abstractions, but are integral to the real world of the mass media—which brings us to the subject of "pluralism," a topic with economic and constitutional ramifications. No one would be much interested in pluralism (whether there is concentration of ownership, for example) if we didn't have some strong notions about the matters of power and control that are related to monopolies. Thus our concern about the "power of the media." And that power is not unrelated to matters of media content—and its "quality." The styles and standards of journalism come into play when we look at "objectivity" and "news-gathering tactics." News decision making is also taken up here. Next, we consider "professionalism" and such methods of media criticism as press councils and codes of ethics. Finally, we confront an issue that is global, but still closely related to many of the others we have explored here—that of "media imperialism."

Readers of the authors' previous books and articles will notice some inconsistencies between those perspectives and what is published here. This apparent inconsistency is inevitable because we are not necessarily presenting our personal viewpoints here, but instead are acting as adversaries and advocates, articulating a "best case" scenario for whatever view we have chosen. For this reason, we hope we are not often quoted out of context.

In preparing this manuscript we are grateful to many of our colleagues and students for stimulating our thinking about communication issues and problems. A special thanks to Professors Vincent P. Norris of Pennsylvania State University, Carol Reuss of the University of North Carolina, and Dwight L. Teeter, Jr. of the University of Texas for their thoughtful comments and helpful suggestions. We are also grateful to our editor at Macmillan, Lloyd Chilton, for his continued encouragement.

This book is designed for college and university courses that go by several names—"Mass Media and Society," "Contemporary Problems in Journalism and Mass Communication," "Ethics in Communication," "Introduction to Mass Communication" and others. We wrote the book mainly for the intermediate student, juniors, seniors, or beginning graduate students. It may also be useful for media history and law courses. Of course, we hope that the communications professionals who are actors in the dramas depicted here will also be among our readers. We believe that anyone who cares about mass communication should be acquainted with the main arguments of the field. We hope this book will help.

E. E. D.
J. C. M.

Foreword

Basic Issues in Mass Communication deserves a place on the book shelf of every newspaper city room in the country.

Though written primarily as a resource book for the teaching of newspaper principles and journalism foibles in journalism courses, this volume is far more than that. It should be must reading for practicing reporters and editors alike.

Professors Dennis and Merrill have crafted a most useful book, one which, in a most effective and painless manner, presses any reader remotely interested in communications to ponder its most common issues and problems.

They present thirteen of these issues, each in a feisty pro and con debate. They selected the right subjects—among them freedom of the press, media–government relations, the people's right to know, access to the press, objectivity, news-gathering tactics, news councils and ethical codes.

The authors' "best-case scenario" method works because of their admitted excessive argumentation. Their technique forces the reader to question, differ, and crystallize his or her own position on the issues.

The book is also successful because the authors write both loosely and informally. Example: One of the gladiators dubs the "invention" of "the right to know" term as a con game; "a great journalistic success of which the media can be proud."

As for the arguments themselves, they are sound and they cover most of the bases, though the writers do not pretend to vintage originality or a complete marshalling of the facts. That is not the point of this volume. The point is to force the reader to think about the basics of journalistic ethics, and it does.

Foreword

As an editor who has been in the trenches for some time, I found *Basic Issues in Mass Communication* a healthy tonic and heartily recommend it to my self-assured brethren as well as to journalism teachers seeking stimulating classroom discussion.

Thomas Winship

Editor, *The Boston Globe*

Contents

Contents

BASIC ISSUES IN MASS COMMUNICATION

Freedom of
the Press

1

Freedom of the press is usually defined as the right to communicate ideas, opinions, and information through the printed word without governmental restraint. A deeply held value in America, press freedom is also legally guaranteed in the free press clause of the First Amendment to the Constitution of the United States. A central purpose of freedom of the press is to encourage the existence of an educated and informed electorate that can make decisions about public affairs. To some early commentators, freedom of the press simply meant the absence of government licensing of printing and publishing. Later it came to mean "no prior restraint" of publication. This is the idea that pre-publication censorship is out of bounds. Freedom of the press is said to assure satisfaction of society's need for a maximum flow of information and opinion and the individual's right for self-fulfillment. Freedom of the press is also a promoter and protector of other rights. In America, a free press is regarded as central to the functioning of democratic government and a free citizenry. There is much continuing debate about the essential nature of this concept of freedom, what it actually means, to whom it extends, whether it is an individual or institutional right. In large part, the contemporary interpretation of freedom of the press hangs on legally sanctioned definitions of such terms as *Congress, no law,* and *press.* Press once meant only the print media, but in an age of broadcast and computer technology, the concept of "the press" has been greatly expanded.

Dennis: The American press is *not* free.

Freedom of the press is one of those noble expressions that slide easily off our tongues, but are not always fully connected to our brains. There is the persistent, romantic notion that freedom of the press flourishes in America and that it is an essential linchpin in our democratic system of government. Many of us want to believe that, but such a belief eludes the truth. The American press is simply not free in any accurate sense of the word. The press fights for freedom and from time to time achieves fragments of freedom, but press freedom is far from full-scale attainment.

I make this argument knowing that the press in America is relatively better off and under less restraint than communications enterprises in many other countries and cultures. I would still argue that bona fide freedom of the press is a distant dream that will probably never be achieved. Why do I say this? Because when all of the romantic rhetoric of press freedom is pushed aside, the most basic formulation of freedom of the press is what the great constitutional scholar Thomas Cooley called, "the right to publish whatever one may please and to be protected against any responsibility for so doing. . . ." Cooley wrote those words in one of the earliest treatises on our constitutional law, but he added this important qualification:

> except so far as such publications, from their blasphemy, obscenity, or scandalous character, may be a public offense, or by their falsehood and malice they may injuriously affect the standing, reputation, the pecuniary interests of individuals. (Cooley, 1868, pp. 885–86).

While Judge Cooley's 1868 statement effectively summarizes the battlefield on which many of the fights for press freedom have been waged, it also is a chilling inventory of exceptions that make freedom quite conditional. And all of Cooley's conditions—except blasphemy— are still alive and well in the trial courts, clearly constraining freedom.

In part, confusion over the idea of press freedom stems from the word *freedom* itself. "Freedom" can be taken to mean the total absence of restraint. The term *liberty* comes closer to Cooley's meaning, because liberty is commonly defined as freedom from all restraints except those justly imposed by law. Liberty of the press assumes a system of rights and duties while freedom of the press does not.

The originators of our legal basis for freedom of the press were the Framers of the Constitution, who were influenced by the Enlightenment philosophers. The Framers inserted the words "freedom of speech, or the press" in what is now the First Amendment. Those simple words unleashed a lively, continuing debate. Two factors that have fueled this controversy are

1. The general lack of agreement about what is meant by freedom of the press.
2. The recognition that freedom of the press does not exist in a vacuum, but instead most coexist with other rights accorded to individuals under the Constitution.

Only the most naive dreamer could look back on the history of the American media and think that they have ever been completely free from restraint. From the earliest times laws were enacted, mainly at the state level, to protect citizens from the press as the Bill of Rights protects citizens from the government and its police. As Cooley suggested those restrictions included libel, (in police terms, false arrest), invasion of privacy, (in police terms, unreasonable search and seizure), and many others. It was generally accepted by society that the press should *not* be free to destroy reputations, undermine the confidence of the community, promote violence, murder, and mayhem, or incite other activities deemed to be harmful. The debate over the extensions (or limits) of press freedom has often centered on whether that freedom is absolute or conditional.

The idea of literal or absolute freedom of the press has found few champions more fierce and steadfast in their views that the late Hugo Lafayette Black, who served on the U.S. Supreme Court from 1937 to 1971. To Justice Black the First Amendment was a literal command. The First Amendment says that "Congress shall make no law ... abridging freedom of speech, or of the press ..." and to Black *no law* meant *no law*. "I am," he wrote, "for the First Amendment from the first word to the last. I believe it means what it says" (Edmond Cahn, p. 53). Although Justice Black (and sometimes his colleague Justice William O. Douglas) was often adamant about the absolute nature of the First Amendment, this position has always seemed silly on the face of it. There are many laws made by Congress and by the state legislatures that constrain and complicate freedom of the press. They range from libel and privacy statutes to laws governing copyright and the publication of government secrets. And even the resolute Justice Black would sometimes admit that at certain times, under certain circumstances and in certain places, there could be limits on freedom of expression. So much for the foundations of First Amendment absolutism. It should also be noted that Black's position on this issue, even when unyielding, was never the view of a majority of the Supreme Court.

Justice Black's brand of First Amendment absolutism is not limited to the lofty chambers of the Supreme Court. I recall encountering this idea, expressed quite vehemently by an editor at the *Milwaukee Journal*. I was speaking to the staff and speculating about some of the trade-offs that citizens expect from the press as a result of the First Amendment franchise. The editor exploded, telling me that there was nothing about that in the Constitution. "*No law,* that's what it says," he told me. "Sounds familiar," I replied.

The philosopher Sidney Hook argues that freedom of the press is not absolute and must yield on occasion to the nation's national security needs or to the rights of individuals that collide with notions of press freedom—for example, the right to a fair trial as guaranteed in the Sixth Amendment or the right of privacy.

There are many complex theories that explore the intricacies of the concept of press freedom and almost all of them agree that press freedom is fragile and volatile, lacking real stability. Some of them point out the negative nature of the First Amendment that figuratively slaps the hand of *Congress* in advance while saying little about what the powerful executive and judicial branches of the Federal government may do. The so-called strong presidency and the "imperial judiciary" could not have been foreseen by the Framers. Some critics argue that the First Amendment really means "all government" instead of Congress per se. Even though the Fourteenth Amendment has been interpreted in such a way that it extends the provisions of the Bill of Rights (including press freedom) to the states, it was not until 1925 that the Supreme Court, in *Gitlow* v. *New York,* told the states not to impair these rights with laws of their own. But even this court ruling and many subsequent decisions that have defined the conditions and contours of so-called press freedom have failed to wipe out a complex series of state and federal laws and court rulings that place severe limits on freedom of the press.

And, if the word *Congress* has caused problems for constitutional scholars, commentators, and critics, the word *press* has been even more troublesome. What, exactly, is "the press"? Only the established newspaper press? Magazines? Broadcasting? Cable television? The lonely pamphleteer? Other forms of communication not yet imagined? Sometimes this problem of defining the press can be a real dilemma. In some cities only "legitimate" newspapers, the more secure majority press, can get press passes, while alternative publications are not regarded as worthy of the unimpeded access to newsworthy events that press passes permit. Since its beginnings broadcasting and later broadband communication (such as cable) have not been accorded the same general rights as the print media. Similarly, filmmakers have long been subjected to various types of censorship.

Most people who have studied freedom of the press agree that one of its fundamental conditions in America is the doctrine of "no prior restraint" of publication. This doctrine holds that the press must be free to publish what it wishes without interference from the government, while remaining subject to various types of legal scrutiny after the fact. This is, of course, a kind of muted freedom, but even here the record is by no means unsullied.

It was the 1931 Supreme Court case of *Near* v. *Minnesota* that struck down a gag law in that state and established the principle of no prior restraint of the press firmly in American constitutional law. However, on a number of occasions since then there have been government attempts to block publication of controversial material. In 1971, for example, the *New York Times* and *Washington Post* published some material about the Viet Nam war from classified government documents two weeks before the Supreme Court conceded their right to do so; in the meantime, the *Times* and *Post* were enjoined from further publication. A similar issue arose with *The Progressive* magazine in 1979 when that publication was prevented for several months from publishing a story about the hydrogen bomb. Now, while there may have been good reason for the government's actions in both instances, they hardly contributed to a sense of freedom from prior restraint. There are scores of examples where courts have placed restraining orders and other gag rules on reporters attempting to cover the judicial system. Again, these restraints may be fully justifiable, but again their presence is *not* press freedom. Of course, such actions are perfectly permissible under our legal system in spite of the First Amendment.

I believe that constraints on press freedom in the public sector by the judiciary, the executive, and the legislative branches of government are only a part of the barrier to freedom of the press in the United States. There are also many restrictions in the private sector. There are elements of contract and property law that severely restrict the press in carrying out its fullest exercise of freedom. There is, additionally, the law of literary property (copyright), which sometimes inhibits republication of particular material. There are many conditions of press ownership that also limit press freedom. The reduced number of voices in the marketplace due to the consolidation and merger of newspaper and broadcast property has effectively scaled down the extent of press freedom. Did New York City have more or less press freedom in the late 1960s when it had seven active daily newspapers than it does today with three? Aren't the manipulative activities of some public relations firms to give their clients low profiles or to obscure the real activities of some companies a limitation on press freedom? Press freedom implies the free flow of information and the right to publish that information. The private sector, often motivated by its own interests, not those of the public, can actively inhibit the flow of information and opinion.

The noble purposes of press freedom as envisioned by the Enlightenment philosophers and others since then would clearly elevate society, but in most instances these are still distant goals, not actual accomplishments, not the reality of the situation today or perhaps ever.

Some commentators say "the structure is the message" in any consideration of media organizations and their behavior. The structure of the newspaper or broadcast organization dictates rules under which reporters and editors operate. There are conventions against certain kinds of behavior. Some stories get covered; some don't. The written or unwritten rules or newsroom policies so fully documented in studies of media gatekeepers are also constraints on freedom. Professionalism itself restrains free will and limits individual choice. Many of us would agree that such private restraints (also called "responsibility" and "ethics") actually limit press freedom, but for the right reasons. There are many forces and factors that have an impact on shaping the performance of the media. They condition and control. They slow and mute freedom.

While there are theorists who believe that freedom of the press has a preferred place in our scheme of individual liberty and freedom, both because of its symbolic primacy* in the Bill of Rights and because of its importance to the functioning of democratic government, the fact remains that freedom of the press, it if exists at all, is engaged in continuous bargaining with other rights and interests, both individual and social. This means that there is what legal scholar Thomas I. Emerson has called "a process of reconciliation" wherein the "rights exercised by one person or one group may be reconciled with equal opportunity for other persons or groups to enjoy them." Thus, we have a complex interrelated system in which rights, principles, practices, and institutions interact. A local newspaper may severely limit my right of privacy today in the name of press freedom, but I might be able to restrain that freedom tomorrow by arguing that pretrial publicity is impairing my right to a fair trial.

The American press lives with rules and regulations, conventions and constraints. By worldwide standards it is *relatively* free, even with all of the limitations on its freedom. It enjoys a measure of liberty and has a mechanism that under most circumstances allows for the adjudication of disputes that constrain freedom. Freedom of the press presupposes the free flow of information and the free dissemination of a wide spectrum of opinions. In most instances we have a rather muted version of this enlightened view of a free press. Even the most perfunctory surface view of the condition of the press in America tells us that it is not really free. A more penetrating look at the many social and psychological influences that have a chilling effect on freedom is a haunting indictment of any claim of press freedom. Finally, as we examine the legal sphere there is a very subtle message that ought to be understood: through the years spokespersons for the press have fought vigorously for greater and greater press freedom.

Some of my journalist friends tell me that "nowhere in the Constitution does it say anything about responsibility; the press has no responsibility to do anything." Perhaps, but the same people are fond of enumerating the rights of the press and the rights of reporters. All *rights,* as anyone who has studied law knows, usually have corresponding *duties.* And any system of free expression which presupposes that there are *rights* also assumes that there are *duties.* Whether these duties are also responsibilities is partly a semantic quibble. However, what appears to be a victory for the press one day, such as the *New*

---

*The no. 1 placement of the First Amendment was actually an accident, not the result of calibrated planning by the Framers.

York Times decision that made it difficult for public officials to sue for libel, later can emerge as a constraint. In a late 1970s Supreme Court case, *Herbert* v. *Lando,* the *New York Times* standard for defining malice ("reckless disregard or knowing falsehood") became the mechanism by which a broadcast producer for "60 Minutes" was required to account for his private thoughts in planning a story. What had been a new right came back to haunt—and also to restrain—the media. Another example is the 1976 case of *Nebraska Press Association* v. *Stuart,* which stopped gagging the press, but led to restrictive orders against news sources.

There are now lengthy inventories of specific rights that the press claims as its own, all won in hard and expensive court battles. While this was going on, one thoughtful champion of press freedom, Alexander Bickel of Yale Law School, observed that the more we have to define freedom, the less freedom we have. This is not inconsistent with Justice Black's view that we should not have tampered with the command of the Framers in the First Amendment. But the fact remains that we have taken considerable license in interpreting its meaning and reach. What remains is hardly a pristine vessel. The charter of press freedom is now somewhat the worse for wear. It is less than whole. It exists mainly in our minds as a social goal, not as a realistic description of the American press today.

Merrill: The American press *is* free.

The preceding argument treats us to the standard absolutist challenge to the concept of press freedom. When we say that America has a free press, of course we do not mean that the press is completely, totally, absolutely free of any and all restraints. Anyone who thinks, even minimally, about press freedom—or any kind of freedom, for that matter—knows full well that freedoms require some kinds and some degrees of restrictions and responsibility.

It may well be, as Professor Dennis has said, that press freedom is a "romantic notion" and that it really doesn't "flourish" in the United States. But that is true with all objectives or goals of a society, and freedom, like "truth," "law and order," "friendship," and "loyalty," is relative, incomplete, and hedged about with inadequacies. And nobody has maintained that press freedom *flourishes* in the United States. Professor Dennis, I feel, exaggerates when he says that the American press is simply not free in any real sense of the word.

The press is indeed free in the commonly understood sense of the word, that in a nonabsolutist, pragmatic, reasonable sense it is free and can be referred to as free. This is, of course, with the implicit understanding that it is not absolutely free of *all* the extrapress and self-imposed restrictions that can easily be brought up by critics.

Even Justice Black and others who have taken basically an absolutist view of First Amendment freedoms have recognized some limitations to press freedom. Obviously, nobody—most of all, the Founding Fathers—has ever considered the press completely free, nor would any sane and responsible person want the press to be.

I am not talking about an anarchistic or nihilistic press; I am referring to a free press—free in the sense of having minimal governmental restraints placed upon it. I am talking about a press in the *real* world of social and political frictions and problems; I am not considering some theoretical level of freedom for an unreal press that might exist in the minds of absolutists and sophists. Just as I might say that the United States is a democratic country (knowing full well that it is not "really" or "totally" so), I can say with assurance and pragmatic validity that America has a "free press."

Of course, as Professor Dennis quotes Sidney Hook as saying, press freedom must yield on occasion to national security. But note that the term "press freedom" is used; and it is this press freedom that "must yield." Such freedom must obviously be assumed (by Hook and by Dennis) in order to be yielded. What American would really want an unyielding concept of press freedom? Reasonable persons, and certainly the Framers of the Constitution were reasonable, would not want an *unyielding* freedom in a nation based on law and social cooperation.

There obviously are, and always have been, a number of factors which keep the American press—or any press—from being totally free. Some of these are external to the press (e.g., considerations of national security, court rulings, libel actions, pressures from advertisers and other groups, and subscriber desires). Some are internal (such as "professional" codes of ethics, the editorial power structure itself, press councils, and the like).

I maintain that the core of press freedom in the United States is editorial autonomy, and that this country's press system can be considered "free" in the sense that it has maximum editorial autonomy—even in the broadcasting aspects of "the press" (those concerning news and commentary, at least). By and large, the American press can make its own editorial decisions and, as a result, can legitimately be considered free. And, certainly, in the context of the press systems of other countries—even those like the United Kingdom and Sweden—it is free. Relatively free, of course, but *free* in a meaningful and realistic sense.

Essentially in the United States there is no prior restraint on the press by government. This means that the media are free to publish or broadcast what they want to without government interference or prepublication censorship. The press can criticize the government without fear of being shut down. This is a key factor. Although, as Professor Dennis has pointed out in his "challenge," there have been a few instances where the courts have instituted some prior restraint on publications, these must be considered exceptions and aberrations; they should not be cited to negate press freedom in America. General statements that are valid are not to be invalidated by pointing to occasional exceptions.

Dennis brings up *newsroom policies* that restrict freedom of the press. Nobody would deny that internal journalistic decision making and management control by the news media's own executives have a restrictive and directive role in journalism. But is this a restriction *on the press?* No. It is, if it is anything, a restriction *by the press*. And it is an inevitable result of freedom of the press. Managers of the press must have the freedom to make their own decisions vis-à-vis editorial content; so they make these decisions, and in so doing are not restricting press freedom, but are *exercising it*.

Freedom does not simply mean "free from." To be free from everything—free from other people, free from laws, free from morality, free from thought, free from emotion—is to be nothing. Unlimited or unrestricted freedom is impossible in fact and should not be demanded by reasonable people. The truth is that any freedom that is possible and desirable does and should have some limitation. Realistic freedom must have some base point or ground.

An example of this grounding of freedom can be found in Confucian ethics. Here the ground or limitation to freedom is goodness. A person should choose good, not evil. If evil prevailed, freedom would probably disappear. Hence, from an ethical perspective, we should permit only the freedom to select good and not the freedom to choose evil. Freedom to choose is only freedom to choose good—not evil. In Confucian ethics, choosing good is the only freedom.

Confucius confirmed this principle in his own life as it related to freedom of speech. He was free to speak as he pleased, and therefore he recognized "freedom of speech"; he would oppose only the speaking of bad words or empty words—that is, words without corresponding actions. Incipient authoritarianism? We have heard the same thing said about Plato, Immanuel Kant, Walter Lippmann, and others. Certainly one might speak of a degree of authoritarianism in Confucius in the same way, and only in the same way, as one might speak of a degree of authoritarianism in Kant or even Jesus Christ. The Categorical Imperative of Kant or the Golden Rule of Christ carry authority, but this authority is self-realized and is in no way externally imposed.

So we can talk about self-determined restrictions *within* an environment of freedom. And still we have freedom—of speech or of the press. A contemporary proponent of ethical restraint, very much a Confucianist in this respect, has been Professor Walter Berns. In his *Freedom, Virtue, and the First Amendment* he issues an articulate call to public virtue. While disassociating himself from intolerance and censorship, he favors, from a moral perspective, certain censorship. Salacious and pornographic publications, he maintains, can be cen-

11

sored. American Communists have no claim to free expression since they are disloyal. Like Confucius, Berns contends that "bad" speakers and "bad" speeches deserve no protection. Government, he believes, should be engaged in raising the moral quality of the community and therefore must judge and limit public discussion according to the moral quality of the writer or speaker. For Berns and others there is a set of moral principles which, though hard to state with precision, are obligatory on all reasonable persons.

Walter Lippmann (see *The Public Philosophy*) would restrict the concept of freedom also—or, more precisely, would have it restricted voluntarily by the individual. Essentially he believed as did Berns: speech and writing, as long as they contribute to the forming of the public mind, should be free. Lippmann believed that the criterion of loyalty is "an indubitable commitment to defend and preserve the order of political and civil rights." To Lippmann and Berns, the disloyal have cut themselves out of the basic agreement that supports the process of public discussion. Lippmann maintains, for example, that there can be no right (freedom) to destroy a liberal democratic state—in this he echoes Plato—and Berns points out that we cannot permit disloyal speech or writing which would generate an American Lenin or Hitler.

So we can see that there have been, and are, thoughtful persons who recognize the necessity of limiting freedom or placing certain moral restrictions on certain forms of communication—whether it is shouting fire in a crowded theater or advocating something that will do harm to national security, public morality, or the continued environment of responsible freedom.

There is, indeed, some danger of authoritarianism implicit in the ideas of these persons. They, like the much-maligned Commission on Freedom of the Press (Hutchins Commission) of the 1940s, are often seen to pose a threat to freedom by stressing responsibility or virtue. And perhaps they do. The debate still rages as to the relative benefits of virtue, responsibility, and social stability over against the benefits of freedom.

We certainly will not get into that at this point, but the reader might like to reassess the pronouncements of John Stuart Mill and others (Locke, Milton, Burke, Jefferson, Voltaire, et al.) who largely base their belief in free expression on utilitarian principles. There is, of course, a relativity and incompleteness to press freedom, but I believe that such qualifications are implicit in the term itself, and that when we think of restrictions on press freedom we are largely thinking about those restrictions placed there by U.S. journalists themselves. By and large, the American press is free to be about as free as it wishes— recognizing, of course, that along with this exercise of freedom comes certain responsibilities and obligations to the society which permits it to exist.

In conclusion, let me reiterate my position. In a realistic sense, there is press freedom in the United States. It is quite legitimate for such a term to be used to describe the American press in spite of the fact that such press freedom is not absolute. The U.S. Constitution protects "freedom of the press"; so there must be something to protect. Journalists think they have press freedom and *what they think they have*, they have. Basically they are speaking of media self-determinism; they are not thinking about limitations and restrictions imposed on them by the press hierarchy itself.

When I say that America has a free press, I am saying that it has a relatively free press, a freer press than perhaps any other country. I am not saying that it has a *completely* free press, nor is anyone else who talks about freedom of the press in the United States. In addition, I am not saying that the media in the United States use their freedom to the degree they might. The freedom is there, but it is not always used. I tend to agree with Philip Wylie when he said

> The image of our media turns out ... to be cowardly and unfree in a very great though not inclusive degree. ... The media, in their mass-circulation or mass-viewed forms, either foster industry's synthetic image, or remain silent about the rot, mess, lies, human debasement, and the rest of the unfavorable truth hid behind the idol. They go along, too, with the support at least by silence, of pious interference with liberty (Wylie, 1969, p. 212).

Philip Wylie is right; not that there is no implication in his words that the American press *could not do better and be freer if it would will to be*. The freedom is there; the fact is that the press often chooses not to use it. Such self-imposed restriction by the press on its freedom does not negate this freedom. It simply sets it temporarily aside until a stronger will, coupled with more courage, will project the press toward a more forceful and responsible utilization of the freedom that it does, in truth, have.

Becker, Carl. *Freedom and Responsibility in the American Way of Life* (New York: Vintage Books, 1960).

Berns, Walter. *Freedom, Virtue and the First Amendment* (Baton Rouge: Louisiana State University Press, 1957).

_____. *The First Amendment and the Future of American Democracy* (New York: Basic Books, 1976).

Brucker, Herbert. *Freedom of Information* (New York: Macmillan, 1949).

Cahn, Edmond N. "Dimensions of First Amendment "Absolutes." A public interview in Dennis et. al., pp. 41–53; see also 37 *N.Y.U.L. Rev.* 549 (1962).

Chafee, Zechariah. *Government and Mass Communication* (Chicago: University of Chicago Press, 1947).

Chamberlin, Bill, and Charlene J. Brown. *The First Amendment Reconsidered* (New York: Longman, 1982).

Cooley, Thomas. *A Treatice on Constitutional Limitations,* Vol. 2, 2nd ed. (Chicago: Callaghan, 1888).

Commission on Freedom of the Press. *A Free and Responsible Press* (Chicago: University of Chicago Press, 1947).

Dennis, E. E., D. M. Gilmor, and David Grey, eds. *Justice Hugo Black and the First Amendment* (Ames: Iowa State University Press, 1978).

Emerson, Thomas I. *The System of Freedom of Expression* (New York: Random House, 1970).

Friendly, Fred. *Minnesota Rag* (New York: Random House, 1981).

Haiman, Franklyn S. *Speech and Law in a Free Society* (Chicago: University of Chicago Press, 1981).

Helle, Steven. "The News-Gathering/Publication Dichotomy and Government Expression," *Duke Law Journal* (No. 1, 1982), 1–60.

Hocking, William E. *Freedom of the Press* (Chicago: University of Chicago Press, 1947).

Lippmann, Walter. *The Public Philosophy* (Boston: Little, Brown, 1955).

Lowenstein, R. L. "Measuring World Press Freedom as a Political Indicator" (Columbia, Mo.: Unpublished Ph.D. dissertation, University of Missouri, 1967).

Luskin, John. *Lippmann, Liberty, and the Press* (University, Ala.: University of Alabama Press, 1972).

McCord, William. *The Springtime of Freedom: Evolution of Developing Societies* (New York: Oxford, 1965).

Meiklejohn, Alexander, *Political Freedom: The Constitutional Powers of the People* (New York: Harper, 1960).

Meiklejohn, Donald. *Freedom and the Public* (Syracuse: Syracuse University Press, 1963).

Merrill, John C. *The Imperative of Freedom* (New York: Hastings House, 1974).

Mill, John Stuart. *On Liberty* (many editions).

Nelson, H. L., ed. *Freedom of the Press from Hamilton to the Warren Court* (Indianapolis: Bobbs-Merrill, 1967).

Pember, Donald R. *Mass Media Law,* 2 ed. (Dubuque, Iowa: W. C. Brown, 1981).

Popper, Karl R. *The Open Society and Its Enemies* (Princeton: Princeton University Press, 1930).

Rubin, Bernard. *Media, Politics, and Democracy* (New York: Oxford, University Press, 1977). See especially Chapter 3—"The Struggle for Media Freedom."

Schmidt, Benno C., Jr. *Freedom of the Press Vs. Public Access* (New York: Praeger, 1976).

Siebert, Fredrick, Theodore Peterson, and Wilbur Schramm. *Four Theories of the Press* (Urbana: University of Illinois Press, 1963).

Stevens, John D. *Shaping the First Amendment* (Beverly Hills, Calif.: Sage Publications, 1982).

Tribe, Lawrence. *American Constitutional Law* (Mineola, N.Y.: Foundation Press, 1978). See esp. Chapter 7.

Wylie, Philip. *The Magic Animal* (New York: Pocket Books, 1969).

Media–Government Relationship

2

The role of government in relation to the mass media is most often stated negatively. Government is commanded by the First Amendment *not* to intrude on press freedom. This command is buttressed by an earlier proposition that the press is a fourth branch of government or a four estate which serves to check on the functioning of government.

The media, especially those involved in public affairs, are said to play a "watchdog" role and thus have an adversary relationship. One of the primary purposes of a free press in a democratic system, it is often said, is keeping the public informed about governmental activities. However, since the media often run into a resistant government, not eager to disclose all, a natural conflict results.

Press probing and revealing and government secrecy and other restraints leads to what has been called, generally by press people, as an "adversary relationship" between government and the press. Some critics say this adversarial relationship has a "checking value" wherein the press checks on government and makes certain that it is performing properly. But another and relevant question is: Who checks on the press and sees that *it* is performing properly? Whether or not such an adversarial relationship actually exists—or should exist—is open to debate.

Merrill: The media and government should *not* be adversaries.

It is commonly assumed in the United States that we have an adversarial media or press system—and what is more, that we *should* have one. The press and government as adversaries is usually seen, at least in the United States, as a proper and necessary relationship. The concept is embraced especially in the rhetoric of journalists.

This concept or assumption is one that needs to be challenged. Granted, many of the hackneyed expressions of American journalism such as the press as a "fourth branch of government," or as a "check on government," or a "watchdog" would tend to solidify such a notion of a press–government adversary relationship, but is it really justified? I believe not. In the argument that follows, I shall try to explain why, first, there is no adversarial relationship under American libertarian theory, and secondly, why the communications media would not want such a relationship to exist.

Why should the press and government be adversaries? Why not friends? Why not foes at times and friends at times? Why, then, should not the relationship be ambivalent—especially in a free and pluralistic press system? These are questions which it would seem unnecessary to ask in the United States. But evidently it is, for the press has taken unto itself the role of an adversary about which it boasts often.

I maintain that theoretically the relationship is not really an adversarial one (the laws are on the side of the press) and should not be an adversarial one—no more than it should be a cooperative and harmonious one. What it should be is an ambiguous one, a free-wheeling one, a changing one. That relationship would be in line with the nature of independent editorial determination, with the spirit of pluralism, and with press freedom.

Beyond this theoretical problem with the adversarial relationship, I maintain that the press does not really want such a pragmatic relationship. The press wants to "adversary" all alone; it basically desires a helpless and law-bound government structure forced to provide the press with anything it wants, with no secrecy on the part of the government, with no attempts to influence or control any activities of the press, with no criticism of the press. What kind of adversarial relationship is this?

Does not press freedom imply, in effect, that any unit of the press system can take any stance it likes toward government? If I am the editor of newspaper A, I may want to consistently support all government policies. I am free to do so. Or I may want to oppose some and support some. Or I may want to never try to point out government weaknesses. I may want to be ambivalent toward government— sometimes pro and sometimes con. I may, indeed, want to determine for my newspaper an *adversarial role vis-à-vis* government, to see my newspaper as a vehicle to fight against government, to check on government, to criticize government, and to make it a policy to root out government excesses and wrongdoing. In short, I may decide to use my newspaper as a "watchdog on government" or as "artillery" with which to bombard government.

In reality, in a libertarian society, the relationship between press and government is so varied and splintered that it cannot be expressed in any monolithic way. It cannot be called *adversarial*. To call it that is a travesty of rhetoric and reality. It is utterly ridiculous for a press to cast itself as an adversary of government: such a stance would imply that the government is always wrong and the press is always right; it would also imply that the press sees itself as an institution dedicated to portraying for the public their government as a flawed, negatively disposed one that must be constantly watched lest it do great harm to the people.

The government, of course, is really closer to the people than is the press, for at least portions of the government are elected by the people. Not so with the press. The press, largely a profit-making private enterprise, has simply set *itself* up as a "representative" of the people and a "check" on government.

In the *Bulletin of ASNE* (May–June 1982), Kurt Luedtke, formerly executive editor of the *Detroit Free Press* and scenarist of the film *Absence of Malice,* courageously aimed some strong words at the American press in this regard. In part he said:

> You [the American press] are forever inventing new rights and privileges for yourselves, the assertion of which is so insolent that you apparently feel compelled—as I certainly would—to wrap them in the robe of some imaginary public duty and claim that you are acting on my behalf. If I am indeed involved, then I would like you to do a little less for me. But of course I'm not. Your claims of privilege have nothing to do with any societal obliga-

> tion, because you have no societal obligation: That is the essence
> of what the First Amendment is all about (p. 16).

Let me follow up this extremely relevant quotation from Luedtke with a brief statement from Paul H. Weaver, associate editor of *Fortune* and *The Public Interest:* "The romantic image of the 'adversary press,' then, is a myth: 'functional' for certain purposes, but wholly inaccurate as a model of what newsmen actually do or can hope to achieve" (Weaver, p. 95).

Traditionally, U.S. journalism has been rather close to, dependent on, and cooperative with, official sources. Undoubtedly this has caused some problems, but it has been one of its strengths. Perhaps at times it has led to some press "cheerleading" for government policies, but it has also maximized the amount of information and disinformation available to the citizens of the country. If I, as a government official, see the press as an adversary, how will I respond to it? With caution, with distrust, with skepticism, with a minimum of openness and frankness, and with a certain hostility. In addition, I certainly will turn my caution and hostility into considerable secrecy and distortion of information I give out to my adversary. Solid and balanced information, therefore, is the victim in this adversarial warfare, with the consumer (the public) receiving the distortions and informational crumbs from the battle.

Further, it seems strange that journalists find any comfort in the concept of an adversarial press. They, if they are realistic at all, should know that they are dependent to a very large extent on government for their news. Virtually all the information published by the journalists about government is derived from (and often validated by) some government-related person. Newspeople know almost nothing about public events and issues except what they obtain from external sources and authorities. If they want to limit or cut off access to such sources, then they will stress their adversarial role; if they want to expand their sources and their information, then they will stress their cooperative and friendly role.

An adversarial role is not a "friendly" role.

An adversarial role is often not even a responsible—or ethical—role. There is nothing sacred or intrinsically good about being an adversary. In fact, adversaries are more likely than not to deal in propaganda—to play games of "disinformation" and "misinformation." Adversaries like to "win"—they are not comfortable with even-handed information, with attempts to inform thoroughly and fairly.

Let us not forget that, in a real adversarial relationship, government has the same right to "fight" as does the press. The government can, in such a relationship, try to withhold information, to have secret meetings, to distort information for its advantage, to have its favorite reporters and reward them in various ways, to deal in disinformation and other propagandistic techniques, to subpoena journalists, and restrict their activities in various ways.

In short, the government would be a true adversary.

The press no doubt does have the upper hand—or would have one—in a real adversarial relationship, unless the Constitution were changed. The press has the last word in any controversy with government. It not only has the last word; it has the first word. The government really has no word at all—except that provided it by the press. Any government official's voice reaching the public through the media is immediately thereafter subjected to "analysis" and "interpretation" by the media figures: telling the American people who have just heard the official what the person "really" said and what he "really" meant. Instant analysis, as it is often called, might better be referred to as "instant bias" by which the press makes sure it has the last word.

The government's hands are largely tied. About the only way it can be an adversary of the press is through occasional verbal blasts at media practices. And these blasts themselves are subject to media control and management and to instant analyses and the "final word" technique. The government, to be sure, does have one other weapon, a purely defensive one—secrecy in certain deliberations. Without a doubt, it makes use of this weapon. But, in the process, it opens itself to more problems: the "leak" by disgruntled functionaries, escalated criticism by the press when it learns of such government operations, the felt need to justify government activities at every turn, and the helpless feeling of government people when the press fires its unanswerable barrages at them.

In a true adversarial relationship, there is one thing the government could do (and should do) to help its position: it should involve itself more in the media business. It should cease permitting the press to be the informer of the people; it should itself actively inform the people, circumventing when possible the commercial press. When the government has no real voice, it is an unequal and almost helpless contender in this press-government fray. Perhaps the Hutchins Commission was correct back in 1947: Should not government, indeed, get into the communications business? It is obvious that in any kind of rhetorical battle, the side without control of internal, public channels of communications is at a distinct disadvantage.

If the people are to know the maximum and to be exposed to the widest range of positions and opinions, it would seem logical that government voices would be of help. In fact, the government probably has a responsibility to communicate directly to the people instead of having its messages filtered through the distorted and often biased lens of the American mass media system. Why should the press, any more than any other institution, be saddled with the awesome responsibility of providing government information to the people?

Surely my coauthor will contend—speaking, I'm sure, for the great majority of press people—that the government has no right competing with private media. But why not *compete?* Is not government competition implicit in an adversarial relationship?

Could not the government through its own publications, broadcast outlets, and other resources fill a multitude of gaps with information and viewpoints? Could not the government then have an instrument to compete with the private media? Could not the government then have a chance to set the record straight—or at least to tell *in its own way* what it has to say to the people? This would be consistent with the concept of pluralism which free press people pay lip service to. It would also make the adversarial relationship more equal. It would give a virtually voiceless entity (the government) a voice with which it could speak directly to its constituency—the people. It would help make it a real contender in this adversarial relationship which actually does not exist at present. An example of this is in Britain where the British Broadcasting Corporation (BBC) competes with independent (private enterprise) networks and stands for quality while still being government-owned.

But, then, as has been noted, the press would not like this. In spite of its talk, the press does not want an adversarial relationship. It cannot really tolerate the thought of the government being its adversary.

The fact that the press looks at itself as an adversary of government is not only theoretically questionable, but it leads to problems with ethics. The belief that the press must be a check on government, a critic of government, or a watchdog on government results in a

22

hyperactive and contentious journalism. The adversarial role causes the press to dig and probe, snipe and snoop; it causes the press to speculate, to deal in gossip and innuendo in its attempt to unearth corruption in high and low places. This press concept is responsible for the press's accentuating the negative in governmental matters, of seldom revealing positive activities. It fosters the idea—or is the creature of the idea—that the government is necessarily and inherently evil and must be checked. And, in this little game which the press sees itself playing, the press has appointed itself to keep the government honest.

Today, as an increasing number of voices are asking who checks the checker, the press falls back on its constitutional freedom guarantee, and when all the rhetoric is done, the answer from the press is essentially this: *Nobody* checks the checker. The press is nearly free from being checked. Is this answer consistent with the contention that the press and government are *adversaries?* There are rare and sometimes celebrated exceptions: Mobil Oil sued the *Washington Post* and won; General Westmoreland took on CBS.

Now, in conclusion, let me quote a reputable American journalist, James Reston, who ends his discussion in *The Artillery of the Press* by contradicting his "artillery fire" title: "Clever officials," he says, "cannot 'manipulate' reporters, and clever reporters cannot really 'best' the government. From both sides, they have more to gain by cooperating with one another, and with the rising minority of thoughtful people, than by regarding one another as 'the enemy.'" So Reston recognizes the mythology implicit in his book's title and in the whole concept of the adversary relationship of the press and government.

Let me repeat my position. There really is no adversarial relationship between press and government and there should not be one.

Dennis: The media and the government *should* be adversaries.

Granted, *adversarial* may be an overlydramatic term to describe the ideal relationship between press and government, but the concept has come to have legitimate meaning and, in fact, as it is commonly understood, it is quite desirable. Adversarial simply means that the media should be critical, argumentative, and contentious in their relationships with government. The press may be the only organizations that have what Justice Potter Stewart called "structural rights" under the Constitution. The primary function of the press under this legal arrangement is to provide the people with a free flow of information.

As anyone who has ever observed governments knows, they try to perpetuate themselves by managing and manipulating information. The press is one of a very few social forces that can challenge such activity through quiet criticism, carping, vigorous attack, and even litigation. From the time of the divine right of kings to the present, government has realized that information is power and the control of information (at least to some degree) is essential to public support for its policies and mandates. This was the reason for the original press licensing and sedition laws in Britain that American colonists and patriots such as John Peter Zenger rebelled against. In modern times governmental secrecy, carried to the extreme, sometimes has deprived the American people of information they needed to be fully knowledgeable citizens. When the White House wanted to cover up the Watergate scandal, the press shouted "foul" and revealed for all to see that seamy chapter in the nation's history. Illegal domestic spying and wiretapping by the Central Intelligence Agency and the Federal Bureau of Investigation have also been uncovered by a vigilant press, wary of government in the best adversarial tradition.

Several of my coauthor's arguments deserve close scrutiny. He maintains, for example, that under a libertarian theory of the press, there is no adversary relationship between press and government. Indeed, the libertarian idea (not to be confused with the Libertarian Party) allows multiple voices in the marketplace and keeps the press as free as possible from government involvement. He is correct in saying that this is strictly up to the editor or broadcaster. Of course, we don't live under a libertarian system today. However, in the late eighteenth and early nineteenth centuries when we did have a libertarian communication system the press fought hard against government strictures on information and helped establish the present adversary relationship. It was during that time (which journalism historians call "The Dark Ages of American Journalism") that the government passed the Alien and Sedition Acts which the press opposed with great fervor. Libertarian journalism brought us highly opinionated, partisan publications. Some were adversaries of government; others were "kept cats," not independent journals, but house organs for political parties. All this ended with the rise of a mass press, which was brought about by a happy mixture of technology, education, advertising, and other factors. Today, while we no longer have a libertarian press system, we do have a press that shares a common value—a critical (or adversarial) posture toward government. What we have is a system of "social responsibility," wherein the press assumes certain rights and corresponding responsibilities or duties. One is the full and robust coverage of government. An adversarial posture is helpful if not essential to this arrangement. One of the only American newspapers I can think of that exemplifies the libertarian tradition is the *Manchester* (N.H.) *Union-Leader,* a fiesty publication known for its biased reporting and vehement attacks on liberal political figures. This paper, operated for many years by the conservative publisher, William Loeb (and presently run much the same way by his widow), sometimes mixes its editorial and news functions. It is clearly a point-of-view newspaper that rejects notions of social responsibility, fairness, and balance. But even the *Union-Leader* has an adversary stance with government, so much so that it can justly be called "antigovernment."

Although it may be somewhat trite, no discussion of the typically American media–government relationship is complete without international comparisons. In so many countries there is a controlled press. Not just in the Soviet Union and China, but also in many developing and industrialized states. In some places, it is not uncommon to have government ownership of the media. Government press councils and laws also limit press freedom. Even in Britain, the mother of democracies, harsh laws, perpetrated by government, keep the media on a short leash. French journalists rightly complain that they could not do vigorous investigative reporting because of the fear of government reprisal.

A call for greater freedom linked to an ambiguous relationship with government is really quite dangerous, even if well intentioned. As should be evident from such recurrent issues as book censorship by school boards, freedom of expression is not something that is established on marble tablets and enshrined for all time. It must be defended repeatedly and continuously or it will cease to exist. Reporters who cover local government often lament their continuing battles with public officials over open meeting and open records practices. The laws regarding public access to meetings and records are on the books, but many government officials will ignore and thwart them unless challenged by the press. Without an adversarial press, it is unlikely that our "sunshine" laws would be used at all. When it comes to such basic rights as press freedom, we must "use 'em or lose 'em."

My coauthor suggests in his opening statement that an adversarial relationship is quite rigid and simplistic while a nonadversarial or "ambiguous" position is more flexible and useful. However, the press need not adopt a single, simplistic posture. It need not have a permanent "mad on," but can have different approaches for different situations. There does not have to be a constant state of war for an adversarial relationship to survive. Even in global affairs, where the U.S. and the Soviet Union are often adversaries, a range of different approaches is used. We are not (at this moment) engaged in a hot war with combat troops, but we have been adversaries through the period of the Cold War, less so during the warming trend of detente, and ambiguously so during the Reagan years of rhetorical hostility and often puzzling economic moves. The same is true with the press and government.

Much like the complexities of Soviet–American relations, press and government in the United States coexist with a mixture of conflict and cooperation. Both are dedicated to the public interest, although they may sometimes see the public interest quite differently. John Kennedy once believed it was in the public interest to withhold information about the U.S. invasion of the Bay of Pigs in Cuba. The *New York Times* did withhold publication long enough for the invasion to occur. Then, after the Bay of Pigs debacle, Kennedy shamefacedly agreed that the *Times* should have published earlier in time to abort the invasion.

Typically, during war or other great national crises, press and government are quite cooperative. The coverage of wars by the press usually supports and does not undermine the government. This accommodation is due both to a conscious practice by the press as well as government censorship which makes coverage difficult and forbids release of information such as that involving troop movements or air and naval maneuvers.

From the standpoint of the pursuit of truth, there is much wrong with slavish cooperation between press and government, even during wartime. This was demonstrated vividly during the Falkland Islands crisis in 1982. The Argentinian press, under the rules of a military dictatorship, was a propaganda arm for the Argentinian cause during that war. The British press was also quite jingoistic, but there was also some critical reporting. The public in both nations got a distorted picture of the truth.

Within the framework of an adversary relationship a whole range of strategies and tactics can be employed by the press and, yes, by government. Washington correspondents, for example, are engaged in an adversarial process. They try to get information about a particular policy or agency. Some of the information is freely provided by helpful information officers; some that might be embarrassing to the agency is withheld or not volunteered. The reporter then develops a strategy to get the missing information. This is done through the use of leaks, alternate sources, or jealous politicians. In this adversary posture the press is suspicious of the actions of government and vice versa.

One of the reasons is that both say they represent the public interest. The government has a strong claim on this title since it operates by the "consent of the governed." The press, on the other hand, is not without some basis for asserting that it is also a representative of the public. At least the press makes this claim in many lawsuits where its motives are challenged. Thus, through court decisions, terms like "the Fourth Branch of Government" and "The Fourth Estate" have gotten real meaning with legal teeth. When the courts, for example, grant the press rights that the rest of us do not have to enter a prison to interview inmates, this special privilege is extended to the press as a "trustee" of the people since we all cannot wander at will within prison walls to find out for ourselves what is happening there. The press does this for us and is, therefore, our representative. Writing in *Saxbe* v. *Washington Post Co.*, Justice Lewis Powell agreed, saying

> The people must therefore depend on the press for information concerning public institutions ... The underlying right is the

right of the public generally. The press is the necessary representative of the public's interest ... and the instrumentality which
effects the public's right [417 U.S. 843, 864 (1974)].

Professor William L. Rivers of Stanford University has documented
in great detail the extent of the adversary relationship between press
and government in two books, *The Adversaries* and *The Other
Government*. He argues forcefully that the press is truly an adversary
of government and has a power base of its own.

The virtues of an adversary relationship between press and government are vividly demonstrated when one compares the news coverage
of public affairs with, say, business or sports. While the coverage of
government is by no means exhaustive (and it assuredly has many
flaws), there is a conscious effort by the press both nationally and in
local communities to cover important events—happenings and issues
in legislative bodies, the courts, and public agencies. At the federal
level the presidency is watched by a legion of several hundred
reporters. A large contingent is assigned to Capitol Hill while very few
cover the Supreme Court and the federal bureaucracy. Look at any
local community and you will see the local press carefully watching the
city council, the courts, and public agencies. This coverage includes
some that is purely descriptive, some is analytical, and some that tries
to ferret out wrongdoing. All of it contributes to an adversary
relationship. Generally, relationships between government sources
and reporters are usually quite cordial. This cooperation is fine when
government is running smoothly and the press is simply doing routine,
descriptive coverage. The more contentious, adversarial stance is
appropriate when things are not going so well and when the public
ought to know about it.

Compare press coverage of government with that of business or
sports. Business coverage has improved markedly in recent years, but
for a long time it was a tedious treatment of commercial activity. Much
of it was little more than the printing of publicity releases which
various businesses and industries provided. The press took little
interest in internal conflicts and controversies or in corporate strategies that led to a particular product line. Since the 1970s, many news
organizations have improved their coverage of business because the
private sector has such a profound impact on individuals and their
communities.

Another area where the press has traditionally cooperated with sources to the extent of becoming boosters and promoters is in sports. Local papers typically support local teams and coaches are lionized by reporters and columnists. Under such coverage many fundamental assumptions about sports in American life which were changing went undetected. Conflicts within sports teams and organizations were neglected or ignored. Sports reporters often did not act like journalists, but more like advocates for teams or players. They ignored embarrassing facts and helped make heroes. Stories involving drug use by athletes, homosexuality, the struggle for recognition by women's sports, and others were "out of sight and out of mind" until an adversarial reporting style was adopted. Today, the adversarial approach is making inroads on sports pages, but progress is slow.

Critics the world over agree that the adversarial relationship makes the U.S. media distinctive. For the most part the press in the U.S. is low key, but on occasion it can rise to greatness by taking on government with a ferocity that can only come when news sources are treated like enemies of full disclosure and free-flowing information. Of course, most of the time this extreme posture is not necessary, but most reporters would argue in favor of a fundamental distrust of government. They might not go as far as I. F. Stone did when he declared that "government always lies," but would agree that it can obscure, distort, and mislead. The public needs an advocate to challenge, cajole, needle, and inquire. In America this is the job of an adversarial press.

FURTHER READING

Baker, C. Edwin. "Scope of First Amendment Freedom of Speech," 25 *UCLA Law Review* (1978), 299.

Blasi, Vince. *The Checking Value in First Amendment Theory* (Samuel Pool Weaver Constitutional Law Series, Chicago: American Bar Foundation, 1977).

Cater, Douglass. *The Fourth Branch of Government* (Boston: Houghton Mifflin, 1959).

DeFleur, Melvin L., and Everette E. Dennis. *Understanding Mass Communication* (Boston: Houghton Mifflin, 1982). See especially Chapter 7, "The News and the Media," for a discussion of changing styles and standards of reporting, including an analysis of adversarial journalism.

Dennis, Everette E. "The Press and the Public Interest: A Definitional Dilemma," 23 *DePaul Law Review* (Spring 1974), 937–60.

Dennis, Everette E., et. al. *Enduring Issues: Mass Communication* (St. Paul: West, 1978).

Franklin, M. A. *The First Amendment and the Fourth Estate.* (New York: Foundation Press, Inc., 1977).

Friendly, Fred. *Minnesota Rag* (New York: Random House, 1981).

Kohlmeier, Louis. *The Regulators* (New York: Harper & Row, 1969).

Luedtke, Kurt. "An Ex-Newsman Hands Down His Indictment of the Press" *Bulletin of ASNE* (651) (May–June 1982), pp. 16–17.

Merrill, J. C. "The Press, the Government, and the Ethics Vacuum," *Communication* (1981), *6,* 177–91.

Porter, William E. *Assault on the Media: The Nixon Years* (Ann Arbor: University of Michigan Press, 1976).

Reston, James. *The Artillery of the Press* (New York: Harper & Row, Colophon Books, 1967).

Rivers, William L. *The Adversaries* (Boston: Beacon press, 1970).

_____. *The Other Government: Power and the Washington Media* (New York: Universe, 1982).

Rourke, F. E. *Secrecy and Publicity: Dilemmas of Democracy* (Baltimore: Johns Hopkins University Press, 1966).

Weaver, Paul H. "The New Journalism and the Old Thoughts After Watergate, *The Public Interest,* No. 35, Spring 1974; also in Dennis et. al., pp. 167–181.

People's
Right to Know

3

Although it is not specifically stated in the Constitution, there is a widely held belief among journalists and other media personnel that there is a "people's right to know." This "right" is usually defined as the right of the public to have access to information about governmental policy and decision making. The press sees itself as the conduit for such information since the average citizen has neither the capacity nor the resources to gather continuing and detailed information abot what the government is doing. The people, the argument goes, must have full and robust information about what their government is doing in order to be knowledgeable voters and good citizens. Government secrecy is thought to lead to suspicion and a lack of confidence in public officials and their policies. The people's right to know is transformed, however imperfectly, from an abstract principle to a concrete reality in "sunshine acts" that require government bodies to hold open meetings and to have their records open for public inspection. Theoretically, government should operate in the open and should be accountable to the people and the "right to know" would make that possible.

Dennis: There is *no* right to know.

The right to know is not an inalienable right guaranteed by the Constitution, but is instead something that was invented by journalists. For a number of years journalistic organizations have been badgering the courts and the legislatures in the hope of establishing their right to access to various confidential sources of information. This so-called "right" now has some modest basis in law, in that on occasion courts have said that under certain circumstances and in very specific areas there is a right to know. But, something so conditional is not a *right* at all, but a quite limited *privilege* that depends on the sufferance of judges. What they give today, they can take away tomorrow. I believe that the right to know is a badly flawed concept that actually interferes with other rights and may do more to impair than to advance First Amendment freedoms.

When journalists (and John Merrill) speak about the right to know, their voices drop into a solemn register. The right to know is most often invoked when media people are asking for rights and privileges that the rest of us do not have. It is a justification for a vague category of corporate rights because the right to know is not put forth as an *individual* right, but as an *institutional* right and here is where the argument gets hazy. The First Amendment guarantees a "right to speak" that belongs to individuals. Advocates of the right to know say that this "new right" is derived from the "right to listen." Listeners (or anyone receiving the messages of free speech and press) are entitled to a flow of information; hence the right to know. This kind of thinking is what we used to call a Triple Wallenda (after the famous circus family who did their tricks on the high wire). It is notable that most of the rights enumerated in the Bill of Rights are for individuals, but our friends in the media would change this by adding a little corporate-institutional appendage.

According to Harvard law professor Lawrence Tribe, one of the leading constitutional scholars, right-to-know advocates would differentiate between the "focused right of an individual to speak" and "the undifferentiated right of the public to know" (Tribe, 1978, p. 674). Professor Tribe says people who take this position argue that the First Amendment does not confer individual rights but protects a system of freedom of expression. "This view," he says, "unduly flattens the First

Amendment's complex role" (Tribe, 1978, p. 675). Another leading scholar, Edwin Baker, agrees. A right to know, he says, is never more than a right to have the government not interfere with a willing speaker's liberty.

Even the most vehement advocates of the right to know (these people use capital letters to make it look and sound terribly solemn and important) admit that the "right" is not to be found in the Constitution; nor do they claim it was specifically thought of or considered by the Framers when they wrote the First Amendment.

The invention of the right to know is a great journalistic success story of which the media can justly be proud. It begins in the early 1950s when the press felt increasingly thwarted by bureaucrats who were standing between them and government information. These journalists wanted access to government records, documents, and proceedings at both the state and federal levels. This was called the Freedom of Information (FoI) movement. The bible for this activist effort was a thoughtful, weighty tome called *The People's Right to Know—Legal Access to Public Records and Proceedings* by Harold L. Cross. Note well the subtitle here, for Cross never advocated an unlimited right to know.

The FoI movement had many positive consequences. It brought sunshine laws (open-meeting and open-record legislation) in most of the states, fostered the Federal Freedom of Information Act, and opened up many governmental meetings from which the press and public had previously been barred. The FoI movement was both necessary and desirable, but the journalists did not stop there. Many excesses would follow.

Over the years the press would claim that it should have access to many classified government records and files, including those dealing with national defense and national security. You will recall from an earlier chapter that *The Progressive* wanted to print the secret of the hydrogen bomb. Journalists also asked for greater and greater immunity from libel suits, both those brought by public officials and by private citizens. Some reporters also told us they should have a right to rummage through the private papers of individuals to "pursue the truth" and frequently claimed that the right of privacy was an undue hindrance on the press and public. One particularly strained argument was made for the journalist's right to get more information out of federal and state prisons through *virtually unlimited* interviews with prisoners. Prison officials disagreed and pointed out that their primary purpose was not running press conferences, but watching inmates. Naturally, the journalists worried more about their desire to interview prisoners than the government's need to maintain control over dangerous individuals who were excluded from society by courts.

So what if journalists argued for these things? If these positions were merely the mutterings of media people at the press club, there would be no problem. But all of these claims and many more were brought to the Supreme Court of the United States. In each case the rationale was—you guessed it—the people's right to know (RTK). This self-serving approach is what Anthony Lewis calls "press exceptionalism": special rights for the press that are not available for the rest of us. This approach also introduces a conceptual problem because the rest of the Bill of Rights applies to individuals, but the right to know is advanced as an *institutional* right. (There are, of course, many dangers inherent in this claim. For example, no one has ever answered the question of whether an institution that has special rights as a surrogate for the public might someday be regarded as a public utility.)

But by this time the RTK folks were not making limited arguments for the release of specific government information, they were trying to establish a broad constitutional right. And, as good lawyers will tell you, there is always "authoritative support" for any position if you look hard enough. In this instance they found it in the writings of James Madison who once said, "A popular government without popular information, or the means of acquiring it, is but a Prologue to a Farce or a Tragedy; or perhaps, both. Knowledge will forever govern ignorance; and a people who mean to be their own Governors, must arm themselves with the power which knowledge gives" (Madison, 1906). RTK advocates could always count on Supreme Court justices Hugo Black and William O. Douglas (when they were alive) to do their bidding. Douglas was particularly eloquent:

> The press has a preferred position in our constitutional scheme, not to enable it to make money, not to set newsmen aside as a favored class, but to bring fulfillment to the public's right to know. The right to know is crucial to the governing powers of the people. (Douglas in *Branzburg* v. *Hayes,* 408 U.S. 665 at 713 [1972]).

This had a bittersweet ring for a number of publishers and broadcasters who are clearly in the communications business to make money and who have only the vaguest, passing interest in the people's right to know, even though their rhetoric sometimes suggests otherwise.

Although the RTK leaders appreciated the support of Justice Douglas, they hankered for something more than mere rhetoric. They thought they had it when, in 1974, Justice Potter Stewart gave a notable speech at Yale Law School. In that now-famous speech Justice Stewart said that the free press guarantee was a "structural provision of the Constitution" and that the "Free Press Clause extends protection to an institution" (Stewart, 1975, p. 631). This is what the RTK people were waiting for: the First Amendment as an institutional right, and mighty support for the idea of a people's right to know. But alas, the "Word According to Stewart" had currency only at Yale. It was not a majority position of the Court (or even a minority view) and thus not the law of the land. The people's right to know was still in the realm of grand theory. Although it has been repeatedly pointed out that the Stewart speech had no standing in the developing law of the First Amendment, it is often invoked as though it were chiseled in stone and blessed by the Framers. This position of structural freedom of the press based on a right to know was and remains one person's opinion and one that has not become a part of the law.

The Stewart speech nevertheless gave much fuel to hungry legal and journalistic minds seeking support for the right to know. The next turn in the debate was a position put eloquently by Federal Judge Irving Kauffman who said that freedom of the press was dependent on protection for three aspects of the communication process: namely, *acquiring, processing,* and *disseminating* information. Now, this makes perfect sense and journalists argued vehemently that it is virtually impossible to disseminate information without acquiring it (through news-gathering methods) and processing it (by editing and preparing for publication). This is logical, of course, but once again journalistic fancy was light-years ahead of legal reality. What Judge Kauffman posited was a theory of freedom of expression and from my point of view a very desirable one, but one without a solid legal foundation. To explain: most legal scholars agree that there is powerful Constitutional support for the dissemination of information. Most First Amendment law centers on the right of people to speak and publish. There is much less legal basis for acquisition of information and, in fact, much of the press's claim in this area is tied to a case which *denied* the press any special journalist's privilege to withhold names of news sources in court proceedings. In that case Justice Byron White offered a less-than-reassuring statement with a double negative construction, that "news gathering is not without its First Amendment protections" (White, in *Branzburg* v. *Hayes,* 406 U.S. 655 at 707 (1972). He did not say what they were. On the matter of processing news or editing it, the law is quite thin. Rarely have courts been asked to give special protection to this aspect of media work and not surprisingly they have not initiated it themselves. In a few instances when they were asked to grant "news-processing" rights, they declined to do so. The press has been inventive and resourceful in trying to establish the right to know as a provision of constitutional law, but to date it has not done so and from all appearances this idea will have to percolate for a long time before it is allowed to raise conceptual havoc with the rather specific language of the First Amendment.

The right to know is a very limited privilege with many important exceptions, so many that to call it a right is misleading. One of the strongest advocates of the right to know is communication law scholar Franklyn S. Haiman, who says the public's right to know is a vital element of the First Amendment "because much essential knowledge is in the hands of agencies and officials of government who can thwart the democratic process by keeping relevant material secret" (Haiman, 1981, p. 368). Haiman says the right to know is based on the need of the public for information to exercise its responsibilities of citizenship and,

> in a fundamental sense, data in the hands of government belongs to the public, having been collected through the use of taxpayers' money and for the exercise of authority derived from the people as a whole (Haiman, 1981, pp. 368–69).

All well and good, but then come the *exceptions* (which Haiman acknowledges and supports) to government disclosures that seriously undermine any "right to know." They are

1. The need to protect the privacy and other legitimate personal interests of those about whom information is gathered.
2. The need to insure candid deliberative processes.
3. The need to safeguard the public's economic interests.
4. The need to preserve the physical safety of society and its institutions (Haiman, 1981, p. 369).

These broad and compelling exceptions blow a hole in the people's right to know, which need not be absolute, but certainly must have a broader reach than Haiman and other scholars envision if it is to be a fundamental right and have real meaning. Rights are not "now you see them, now you don't" propositions.

The right to know, then, has a flimsy legal foundation, which is reason enough to question whether it should be accorded the kind of status journalists want to confer upon it. But there are even more compelling reasons for viewing this so-called right with real trepidation. Journalist and screenwriter Kurt Luedtke, whom we have quoted elsewhere in this book, put it succinctly in a 1982 speech when he told the American Newspaper Publishers Association that

> There is no such thing as the public's right to know. You made that up, taking care not to specify what it was the public had a right to know. The public knows whatever you choose to tell it, no more, no less. If the public did have a right to know, it would then have something to say about what it is you choose to call news. (Luedtke, 1982, pp. 4–5)

Luedtke is right. If the public really does have a right to know, it surely has a right to determine what information it truly needs to know and to demand that the press (as its surrogate) deliver that information forthwith. Out the window goes the right of the editor and broadcaster to edit and to decide what is news. And here the nightmare begins. If the press is to become the legal representative of the people under a general principle of a right to know, then it will certainly be told by the courts and legislatures that it has a duty to provide particular information to the public. This definitely would be a shocking intrusion on freedom of the press and is something that I would hope no thinking journalist would advocate. New rights bring new duties and I have serious doubts that the press will want the baggage that will come with the public's right to know, if such a right should be given full and complete constitutional protection. I say let well enough alone, stop making self-serving claims in the name of this public "need."

Merrill: There *is* a right to know.

Professor Dennis contends that the right to know is not an inalienable right guaranteed by the Constitution, and that it is, rather, something invented by journalists. It is difficult to dispute either of these contentions. Such a "right" is not overtly in the Bill of Rights, and it does seem that only journalists have made much if anything of such a right.

Nevertheless, even after saying this, I must insist that a right to know for the citizenry of a libertarian society (free and open) does indeed exist—even if such a right is a philosophical right and not spelled out literally in the First Amendment.

It may well be that a people's right to know is not explicitly stated constitutionally, but journalists did more than "invent" it; they inferred from the "freedom of the press" clause that a people's right to know existed. I suppose that by making such an inference, which seems quite logical to me, they did in a sense *invent* this right to know. But instead of feeling guilty for such an "invention," if such it was, journalists should be proud of the fact that they have seen this public right standing in the philosophical shadows supporting a free press.

Why, we should ask, should the Founding Fathers provide for a free press? Simply for the sake of having a free press? Just so future citizens could brag about such a provision? Obviously there was a pragmatic reason for the free press (as well as the free speech) provision in the Bill of Rights. And this reason revolves around what we now call the people's right to know. If the people of the republic (the sovereign rulers of the country) do not know about public affairs and government business, they surely cannot be good sovereigns; they cannot govern themselves well. They, in the philosophical framework they find themselves in, *must* know. Their government is built upon the assumption that they will know; therefore, certainly it is their "right" to know. They need to know; they have a philosophical mandate to know in order to be consistent with their political purpose. The very reason for a free press is that the people can know.

Someone will ask: If the people have a right to know, then does not the press share responsibility with government in letting them know? My answer is yes. If the press argues for such a right (and I maintain that the press in a free society with its press freedom *must* believe in such a foundational right), then it must take very seriously its responsibility of providing knowledge about public affairs to the people. If there is such a public right to know, and I believe there is, then the press has an important responsibility to fulfill this right—to see to it that the people are able to know.

At this point the government enters the picture, for the press cannot let the people know what it (the press) cannot get from government. So, I maintain that the people do have a right to know public business and that both the press and the government have the responsibility to let the people know. Certainly the people cannot know about their government without the cooperation of both press and government. Just because the press and government both fail, from time to time, to let the people know does not eliminate the people's right.

The concept of "the people's right to know" has mainly been promoted since World War II; books such as Kent Cooper's *The Right to Know* and Harold Cross's *The People's Right to Know* and numerous articles have been printed declaring such a right and castigating government for infringing on it. No adherent to a libertarian theory of the press can but admire and applaud such antigovernment broadsides, but the problem is larger than this.

Two other important factors are involved in this business of letting the people know: the *people* and the *press*. Too often they are left out of a discussion of this topic.

Frankly, the people either don't know they have a right to know or they don't take it seriously. It appears that they simply don't care. Such a right to know is certainly one of great importance—a civil right if there ever was one. Such a right is at the very foundation of American government, of public discussion, of intelligent voting, of public opinion, of the very fabric and essence of democracy. And yet the people appear to have little or no concern for this right. But— unconcern does not do away with the right.

The only segment of our society that seems really concerned about the people's right to know is the press. Journalists criticize, agitate, and fret about the "people's right to know" being infringed upon by government. They justify—rightly—their own press freedom by appealing to the public's right to know.

A problem with the press is that it places all the blame on government for denying the people this right. This, of course, is not true. The news media themselves participate in the denial of this right. Any person familiar with the typical news operation must recognize that only a very small portion of government-related information gets to the average citizen's eyes or ears. So, in effect, the news media are themselves guilty of the same sins of omission and commission that they point to in government.

Editors and news directors, while promoting the idea of a people's right to know, are busy selecting and rejecting government information. They leave out this story, that picture, this viewpoint. They play up this speech, trim that one and put it on page 44, leave another one out completely, and on and on. They are, in effect, "censors"—perhaps with the best of motives, but "censors" nevertheless. They manage the news also, just as government officials do. They play their parts, too, in the restriction of the people's right to know.

Of course, editors call this practice "exercising their editorial prerogative." They see themselves as "editing"; they see the government people as "managing" and "restricting" public information. But the people's exercise of the right to know is being limited regardless of these semantic games.

All the while the press people are hailing the "right to know" as indispensable for the country.

One who observes the editing operations of a newspaper or magazine is struck by the swiftness with which government news is discarded. And, when the wastebaskets fill with the information that the people presumably should be reading, it will be noted that there are few tears and there is little gnashing of teeth in the journalistic ranks. It is as if these practitioners of journalism obscure their own coverage of government without even realizing that they, like the government officials they criticize, are keeping back information that, in their own words, "the public has a right to know."

The media people are right, of course. The public does have a right to know. This right has always been in the American journalistic context even though it has not been traditionally as popular as it has been since World War II. Now the emphasis is shifting from the press to the people, from journalistic freedom to journalistic responsibility, from institutional rights of the press to social rights of the citizenry. It is all part of the shift from "negative freedom" to "positive freedom"—from freedom *from* to freedom *to*. Part of the social responsibility theory of the press is an emphasis on what the press *does* positively, not what the press might be kept by government from doing.

The people's right to know is a logical outgrowth of this trend. I maintain that the philosophical rationale for press freedom (interpreted until recently as the *press's* freedom) all along has been that *the people need to know*. This need philosophically is translated into a "right" in our type of pluralistic, open, libertarian society where the people theoretically are the sovereigns.

So, in spite of the sophisticated arguments put forward by Professor Dennis and others who deny this people's right, I propose again, in conclusion, that such a right exists. However often it is denied the people—by government and by the press—it is still there serving as the main underpinning of a democratic society of the American type. It is the justification for press freedom and the absolute requirement for the political viability of the United States.

Anderson, Jack. "We the People: Do We Have a Right to Know?" *Parade* (January 30, 1966), 4–5.

Boyer, John H. "Supreme Court and the Right to Know" (FoI Center Report 272, University of Missouri, November 1971).

Cooper, Kent. *The Right to Know* (New York: Farrar, Strauss and Cudahy, 1956).

Cross, Harold L. *The People's Right to Know—Legal Access to Public Records and Proceedings* (New York: Columbia University Press, 1953).

Dennis, Everette E., D. M. Gillmor, and David Grey, eds. *Justice Hugo Black and the First Amendment* (Ames: Iowa State University Press, 1978).

Douglas, William O. *The Right of the People* (New York: Doubleday, 1958).

Haiman, Franklyn S. *Speech and Law in a Free Society* (Chicago: University of Chicago Press, 1981).

Luedtke, Kurt. "The Twin Perils: Arrogance and Irrelevance." American Newspaper Publishers Assn. Convention, San Francisco, 1982.

_____. "An Ex-Newsman Hands Down His Indictment of the Press," *The Bulletin of ASNE* (May–June 1982).

Madison, James. *Writings of James Madison,* G. Hunt, ed. (1906).

Merrill, J. C. "Is There a Right to Know?" (FoI Center Report 002, University of Missouri, January 1967).

_____. "The People's Right to Know Myth" *New York State Bar Journal* 7 (November 1973), 45.

_____. "The Press, the Government, and the Ethics Vacuum," *Communication* (1981), 6.

Rourke, Francis E. *Secrecy and Publicity: Dilemmas of Democracy* (Baltimore: Johns Hopkins University Press, 1966).

Schauerte, Bud. "Yes, There Is the Right to Know" (FoI Center Report 003, University of Missouri, May 1967).

Schwarzlose, Richard A. "For Journalists Only?" *Columbia Journalism Review* (July/August 1977), 32–33.

Spangler, Raymond. "You Have a Right to Know—What?" *The Quill* (February 1970), 4.

Stewart, Potter. "Or of the Press," *Hastings Law Journal* 26 (1975), 631.

Time essay. "The People's Right to Know: How Much or How Little?" *Time* (January 11, 1971), 16–17.

Tribe, Lawrence H. *American Constitutional Law* (Mineola, N.Y.: Foundation Press, 1978). See especially, Chap. 12, "Communication and Expression," pp. 576–736.

Whalen, Charles W., Jr. *Your Right to Know* (New York: Vintage Books, 1973.

Williams, Lord Francis. "The Right to Know," *Twentieth Century* (Spring 1962), 6–17.

Public Access to the Media

4

The principle of public access to the media is based on a positive interpretation of the press clause of the First Amendment. The clause ("Congress shall make no law . . .") is, of course, stated negatively. Under a positive interpretation it is often claimed that the public has a right to freedom of the press through access to the media, that is, through a right to publish opinions and be heard in the printed press and on broadcast stations.

It is maintained that the public has no real freedom of the press without this right of access; only those who own the means of communication have freedom of the press. (The counterargument is that in order to have freedom of religion, speech, or assembly, one need not own a church, a public platform, or a street.) The theory of access posits that the First Amendment grants protection to all persons, not just those who own the mass media. The right of reply to newspaper and broadcast material and the right to buy advertising have been suggested as corrolaries to the right of access.

Merrill: The public has *no* right of access.

Many critics of the press for the last several decades have proposed that the First Amendment should be reinterpreted so as to force the mass media to give space and time to individuals and groups wanting to present "minority" points of view. One key leader in this crusade for a "right of access to the press" has been Professor Jerome Barron. He has argued that the First Amendment prohibition on government restraint does not forbid the government from acting to enhance citizens' opportunities to exercise their freedom of (to?) the press. He has argued vigorously in favor of a legal right of access to the mass media by citizens.

In the June 1967 *Harvard Law Review* and subsequently in many other articles and speeches, Barron has proclaimed that the main interest of media owners and controllers is to maximize profit, not discussion. Only with a right of access to the press, Barron argues, can the voice of the people be heard. What he and others of similar belief are advocating is a new interpretation of the First Amendment whereby the courts can mandate use by the press of material from individuals and groups.

This key passage from Barron's original *Harvard Law Review* article provides the thrust of the "access" position:

> Our constitutional theory is in the grip of a romantic conception of free expression, a belief that the marketplace of ideas is freely accessible. But if there [ever was] a self-operating market place of ideas, it has long ceased to exist. The mass media's development of an antipathy to ideas requires legal intervention if novel and unpopular ideas are to be assured a forum.

And in an article in the March 1969 *Seminar,* law professor Barron drove home his main thesis:

> The mandate for a free press is not a constitutional gift to publishers alone. The reader, the public, and, in a larger intellectual sense, the world of ideas all have a stake in the press. That indeed is the reason for the special status of the press in the United States (Barron).

The courts have not been impressed with Barron's arguments so far,

46

although the topic has become popular in public and journalistic debate. The firmest rejection of Barron's arguments came in the *Tornillo* case in Florida. In the fall of 1972 Pat Tornillo, Jr., a candidate for the Democratic nomination in a Florida state legislative primary, sought to use a 1918 state law saying that a newspaper assailing a candidate's character had to give that candidate a chance to reply free of charge. The *Miami Herald,* having carried a critical editorial about Tornillo, nevertheless refused to provide free space to Tornillo to answer it. Tornillo and Barron, who was Tornillo's legal counsel, convinced the Florida Supreme Court of their position, but the U.S. Supreme Court took the view that editorial decisions were to be made by editors, not courts.

If an individual citizen (such as Tornillo) should have the right of access to a newspaper, then why should not the government have a similar right? Why should not President Reagan, for example, have the right to force the *Washington Post* to print his answer to a critical editorial? Why would not any government official have such a right to get his (or his agency's) side into the press? It is hard to imagine the chaos that would result from such a situation, with editorial decisions of this type being made in the already overloaded courts. The editors of the country would find themselves mere figureheads, making no editorial decisions—or feeling the "chilling effect" of such a legal system to such a degree that they would fill their columns with material from those they feared most might take them to court.

Barron may have seen his suggestion as a new "interpretation" of the First Amendment. I see it as a perversion of or abdication from the First Amendment. It so obviously takes away editorial freedom or determination (by the press) that it should strike any reasonable person as a travesty on the concept of press freedom. In essence, if individuals could force their opinions into newspapers, newspaper editors would lose their freedom to use or reject an article; any editorial determination would obviously be gone.

No one will deny that there are persons in the public who would like to have access to the large audiences reached by the major mass media. Naturally I have opinions; I have certain messages I would like to see made public in a newspaper like the *New York Times* or my local daily. Naturally, a certain limitation is placed on me if I cannot get my opinions published. I still, however, can *speak* my opinions, whether or not my voice reaches all the hearers I might like. My right of free speech is not negated just because I do not have as large an audience as

I would like. The fact that there is a freedom of speech clause in the First Amendment as well as a free press clause indicates to me that the writers of the Bill of Rights intended to separate the two: that there would the press's freedom of the public prints *and* the people's freedom to speak. If not, there would have been no need to state both rights in the First Amendment.

It is, in fact, relatively easy for people with something to say today to get their ideas (or some of them) before the public or portions of it. But, say the "access" people, the problem is getting a big audience for the message. The important thing, they say, is getting one's message into the mass media—newspapers, magazines, radio, and television. This, of course, is a natural desire for anyone who thinks he has something important to say. But I agree completely with Ayn Rand in her position on this matter. She is in opposition to those, like Barron, who would "redefine" the First Amendment as giving "the people" some kind of inalienable *right* to have someone else publish their opinions.

> The right of free speech means that a man has a right to express his ideas without danger of suppression, interference, or punitive action by the government. It does *not* mean that others must provide him with a lecture hall, a radio station, or a printing press through which to express his ideas (Rand, 1964, p. 97).

With Rand, I believe that there are no "rights" for consumers of journalism if no journalist chooses to produce those particular kinds of journalism certain consumers *want*. There is only the right for any citizen to be a journalist and produce them himself—or for him to *try* to get the kind of journalism he desires, or to *try* to get his ideas into the journalistic media.

"Remember," writes Ayn Rand, "that rights are moral principles which define and protect a man's freedom of action, but impose no obligations on other men." A case in point would be Rand's own book in which these words appear; she had the freedom to write, but it was a publisher who decided that her views were of sufficient interest to warrant publication.

Let us consider a basic question: *Who* are the editors or editorial decision makers in the American press system? Who *should* be? Are they persons working for (or owning) private newspapers—or are they some outside authority? This is a question that cannot be turned aside with idealistic arguments about some theoretical "people's freedom," the desire on the part of individuals to have their opinions published. The concept of "people's freedom" is suggestive of the socialist world's emphasis on a "people's press." Even a cursory knowledge of the press of a country like the Soviet Union exposes what happens to "press freedom" and pluralism when the rhetoric of a "people's press" is actually put into practice.

I fail to see how the Founding Fathers had in mind any concept of the *people* (nonprinters and nonpublishers) having "freedom of the press." The concept is utterly ridiculous when applied to the press, both from a philosophical and from a linguistic perspective. When the First Amendment was written, the writers had in mind prohibiting the control and suppression of the press by a government such as that prevailing in England; they did not want such a situation to exist in the Colonies. They wanted the *press,* not the government, not the courts, to make editorial decisions. They were trying to head off any *a priori* press censorship or control by government.

I believe that when the Colonial leaders spoke of the "press," they meant the press; they did not mean "the people." When they wanted to talk about the people, they spoke of the people. If they had considered the Barron contention that the people should have a right of access to the press, they would have clearly placed that "right" where it belonged—in the Bill of Rights. Certainly they would not have obscured such a right under the free press right; it would have been much too important for such linguistic games. If the people were to have the right to force their messages and opinions into the papers of the colonies, then this would have been a "right" so important that it would have had to be explicated (or at least listed) in the Bill of Rights.

If one looks at this complex issue as having to do only with assuring minority opinions a fair hearing, it is little wonder that a proposal like Professor Barron's would be considered salutary and perhaps even long overdue. This, however, is not where the problem ends. If such a proposal were taken seriously by enough powerful people in the country to bring it into practice, a whole new bag of troubles would be opened to plague the person concerned about protecting a free press. Even as "freedom of the press" implies the freedom to be heard—a freedom for the consumer—we must not forget that it also implies the freedom to print or not to print—a freedom for the publisher.

The First Amendment provides that Federal government *will not pass any laws* which abridge press freedom. Although press freedom is not defined in the Bill of Rights, an explicit concern with not passing laws which might diminish press freedom appears to be quite clear. When any group—even government seeking to remedy certain ills which it believes it detects—tells a publisher what he must print, it is taking upon itself an omnipotence not far removed from authoritarianism. It is restricting press freedom in the name of freedom for an individual to have an outlet for his messages and in the name of freedom to read.

This paradox brings up the interesting point that "freedom of the press" should not be used synonymously with "freedom of information." It is obvious that the press can have freedom to print anything it desires without making available to the reader everything it has available to print. Its freedom, in other words, imposes an implicit restriction on the reader's freedom of access to every bit of information or point of view.

Looking at it in this way, it is not difficult to see that press freedom does not imply freedom of information. The latter term refers to the right of the reader to have all material available for reading, while the former term denotes the right of the publisher to publish or not to publish.

Perhaps the problem is that we try to make the term "freedom of the press" cover too much. If we were to understand it narrowly, in the sense clearly indicated by its syntax, we would emphasize the *press* and its *freedom* in the context of information flow. This would mean that "freedom" belongs to "the press." The press alone, in this definition, would be in the position of determining what it would or would not print. The press would have no prior restrictions on its editorial prerogatives; this would be *press freedom*. Those who favor an interpretation of the First Amendment that protects "freedom of information" would hardly agree to a definition that de-emphasizes the rights of "the people."

The vision of a better journalistic world through coercive publishing rests mainly on the assumption that important minority view-points are not being made known in the United States, and that this is deleterious to a democratic society. Although I will not challenge this main premise here, it seems incumbent on those who advocate controlled access to name some of the important minority positions that are not being publicized by the American press.

The person who is concerned about what is *not* in the press does not appear to be concerned primarily about the *freedom of the press* to make editorial decisions. However laudable this concern may be, we must recognize that such a position is potentially *authoritarian,* just as the existing libertarianism of the press is potentially *restrictive.*

Those who would compel publication justify their position by using terms such as "the public's inherent right to be heard," and the "public's right to know," and "press responsibility." Thus such people put what they regard as the social good above what individual publishers consider their right of editorial self-determination.

Few thoughtful individuals would quarrel with the position that "the good of society" or "social responsibility" are laudable concepts that should be served by the press. However, trouble comes when these theoretical concepts are applied to the actual workings of the press in society. The *what* of the concept presents considerable difficulty. What, for instance, is the best way to do the most good for society, and what is the best way to be socially responsible? There are many who would feel very strongly that forcing opinions (especially "certain" opinions) into a newspaper would be very harmful to the "social good," and that this would be the epitome of social *irresponsibility.*

The *how* of the concept adds further complications. How will decisions be made about what shall or shall not be printed? What would be a rational manner of making such determinations if we are to take them out of the hands of individual publishers and editors? A federal court? A federal ombudsman? A FPA (Federal Press Agency) organized on the lines of the Federal Communications Commission?

Among all the "minority" positions in a given community or in the nation, which ones would have a "right" to be published and which ones would not? Which spokesman for any one "minority" would be published as a representative of the whole minority? Or would all of them—or many of them—be published, since undoubtedly there is a pluralism in minority opinions even on a single issue? These are basic and important questions—questions that would constantly plague the *authority* that would have to make such decisions.

This would take us back to the same situation that exists with editors or publishers making the decisions as to what to use and not to use. Viewpoints that one court (or authoritative body) would deem valuable and thus worthy of publication might, to another authoritative body that is equally perspicacious and dedicated, seem inane, irrational, or otherwise lacking in value. Undoubtedly, even among the staunchest advocates of minority rights there is preference for *some* minorities over others. How will such a system differ really, in any substantial way, from variances of decisions presently made by editors? One thing is certain: not every opinion can be used. Somebody has to make the editorial decisions, be it editor or court or other entity. Therefore, always there will be the charge by someone that he is not given the proper exposure for his opinions.

Beyond this, there is another perplexing and closely related problem. What emphasis should various minority views receive in the press, or even in a single newspaper? Would this be decided by the proportion of the total population which the "minority" under consideration comprises? Would it be decided on the basis of the "worth" or "intrinsic value to society" of the viewpoint espoused? If so, how would such worth be ascertained? Would it be decided on the basis of the economic or political pressure which a particular person or group might bring to bear on the power structure? How would a nonpress decision on what will or will not be printed have any real advantages over pluralistic editorial decisions made by the press itself?

Many persons will reply that these are unimportant and theoretical questions that should not be permitted to interfere with the serious consideration of a forced-publishing system. Sure, they will say, there will be problems and weaknesses, but we must push on in spite of obstacles toward a New Journalism in which all opinions receive equal and just airing and no minority group or "aggrieved" individual can feel slighted by the treatment received in the press.

I maintain that proposals for the right of public access or for a legally forced publishing concept, in spite of idealistic objectives, are extremely naive in view of the practicalities of day-to-day journalism and the explicit language of the Bill of Rights.

Dennis: The public *has* a right of access.

On its face this may seem to be a difficult, if not impossible, position. However, it is not. Many opponents of the right of access say the issue has already been decided in the *Tornillo* case. Did the Supreme Court of the United States demolish access in its 9–0 decision striking down the Florida law? No, not quite, but unfortunately for access advocates, Jerome Barron, who was an attorney for plaintiff Tornillo, used the case albeit a weak one to test the theory of access. He lost but that loss does not forever pull the chain on the right of access.

Public access to the media is based on a quite simple and, I believe, just assumption: that when the Framers of the Constitution wrote the First Amendment, they meant that *all* the people have a right to freedom of the press, not just the *owners* of the media. Professor Barron worries that a "romantic and lopsidedly propublisher" (Barron, 1973, p. 12) view of the First Amendment does not necessarily benefit the public. When we look closely at other features of the First Amendment, the interpretation that only the owners of the media can enjoy press freedom seems strange indeed. Press people often forget that the First Amendment also says something about religion, speech, and assembly. Consider freedom of religion, for example. No one would sensibly argue that *only* organized religious groups or churches have freedom of religion. On the contrary, we understand that both individual and institutional rights (i.e., those of churches) to freedom of religion can be accommodated under the First Amendment. The religious rights of individuals have been tested repeatedly in the courts and, over time, a substantial legal basis for them has been developed.

Very few cases involving individual rights to press freedom have gone to the courts and there is little formal legal foundation for a people's right of access. This should not deter us from pursuing the case for access. After all, there was no legal assurance for a right of privacy in 1890 when Samuel D. Warren and Louis Brandeis wrote a famous law review article proposing it. In time, the right of privacy was articulated in statutes, court decisions, and philosophical treatises. Today few would question that there is such a right. Indeed, there is both a tort(s) of privacy and a constitutional right of privacy. Similarly, Professor Barron is ahead of his time in arguing for a legally protected right of access.

While it is true that the Framers did not specify people's rights, it can be argued that they did intend the provisions of the Bill of Rights to apply to individuals. Institutional rights (such as those extended to the press as an institution) are granted because they have responsibilities to individuals, to citizens who can benefit from the activities of the press. The role of the press, then, is to deliver press freedom to individuals, communities, and the country. A country is the sum of its parts and its parts include individuals. The Framers expected the press to promote the free flow of information. Is that free flow one-way only or should the press be responsible to its audience? Should it meet people's informational needs? Should it reflect and report on their opinions and ideas? The answers, I think, are a resounding "yes." But just how this should be accomplished and whether a right of access is the best way needs considerable analysis and study.

In spite of some harsh things said about him, Professor Barron is hardly a dangerous radical. A law school dean and distinguished legal scholar, he simply believes that all people should have a legal right to buy advertising and be able to reply to editorials which either mention them or affect them directly. This is a modest request and a step toward allowing the public to talk back to the media in an age when mass communication plays a central role in their lives.

Barron and others in the access movement would not turn the news media over to a howling mob and strip editors of their legitimate right to make editorial decisions. Barron's two proposals would require enabling legislation in states and perhaps in Washington. Then, that legislation would no doubt be tested for constitutionality by media groups opposing it. If it met the test, there would be a guaranteed public right of access.

It has long been assumed that by granting freedom to the *issuer* of communication (the media), quite naturally the *user* (the public) also had press freedom. This was the view of the distinguished philosopher William Ernest Hocking, who was a member of the Commission on Freedom of the Press. "There are," he wrote, "two distinct interests ... only one of them needs protection; to protect the issuer is to protect the consumer" (Hocking, 1947, p. 164). Freedom of the press, he suggested, "has always been a matter of public as well as individual importance. Inseparable from the right of the press to be free has been the right of the people to have a free press."

It seems to me that this is a specious position. There can be a perfectly free press, but it may be so elitist that it traditionally speaks to and for a limited segment of the population. Indeed, in America today, market researchers advise media executives that certain people are not worth communicating with because they have limited ability to buy the products being promoted through advertising. For years, minority persons in the United States were "the invisible Americans." Their views, problems, and concerns were simply not covered by major media. This lapse became quite evident during the demonstrations, marches, sit-ins, and riots of the 1960s when many disenfranchised people took to the streets. In fact, as a result of the upheavals, American media leaders agreed to provide (a) more complete and extensive coverage of minority communities and (b) jobs in the newsroom for minority persons. During the social upheaval of the 1960s there were several reports on the press that criticized the media for turning their backs on the problems of minorities. In the early 1980s, a Brookings Institution report pointed out that some of America's most popular tourist cities—Boston, Philadelphia, and St. Louis—were in worse shape than less glamourous places like Detroit and Newark. How could this be? "There are two Bostons," wrote one newspaper columnist:

> There is the Boston which civic leaders take great pride in and love to show off to visiting dignitaries . . . its booming hotels and offices, its revitalized downtown, and showcase waterfront development. And there is the other Boston, with its poverty, crime problems, racial prejudice, deteriorated housing stock, unemployment, educational problems, poor fiscal condition, and troubled transportation system.

And, he might have added, only one Boston finds its voice and its views in the major newspapers and television stations, the other does not.

Two distinguished researchers, Floyd Mattson and Jim Richstad, assert that not only are people entitled to freedom of the press, but that there is an inherent "right to communicate." Other scholars agree that self-expression is one of people's basic needs and it would follow that there ought to be some mechanism for this in a civilized society. It would also seem that there will be a great benefit to society if people's sense of powerlessness can be reduced and partially satisfied by letting them have a forum for their ideas, complaints, and frustrations. There are some opportunities, of course, in newspaper letter columns and radio and television call-in shows, but they are minimal given the potential demand. If we can agree that there is a fundamental right to communicate and that the Constitution means everybody should enjoy freedom of the press, then it should not be impossible to develop a regime wherein such freedom of expression could be encouraged. It could occur in at least two ways:

1. Through natural forces of the free market place.
2. Through governmental intervention and mandatory access where appropriate and necessary.

In the first instance, I would see advocates of access in the private sector mobilizing information campaigns to help people use the available channels of expression, those mentioned above and others. In addition, it may take reminders from access leaders to leaders of the media to point up the value both commercially and socially of staying in touch with all aspects of the community.

Individuals and institutions or neighborhoods that are being systematically or routinely ignored in news coverage should fight back by competing for their fair share of media attention. This can be done with various strategies and regular information campaigns. The commercial advantage to the media of staying in touch with particular market segments can be emphasized as well as the social obligation to reach out to all elements of the community. Many editors would respond affirmatively to such an approach. And they would likely provide space on the editorial page for occasional columns and commentaries. The same could be done with television and radio.

Perhaps the most significant development on the public access front is cable television. As America is wired for cable in the 1980s and 1990s, many local cable operators are providing public access time for use by local citizens. In cities where public access has been tried it has enjoyed a degree of success. Access in this instance is an umbrella term for free, noncommercial channel time that a cable operator makes available for use by public agencies, nonprofit organizations, and private citizens. Under most franchise agreements, the cable operator provides studio facilities, cameras, and editing equipment. Cable public access has existed in New York City since 1970 and there is a track record of high use by individuals, especially persons from the black community who had a difficult time getting on commercial television. Public access gives ordinary people a chance to participate in the marvels of the electronic age as well as to be heard by their fellow citizens. Although public access channels are not particularly popular with commercial cable television operators who would rather put revenue-producing fare on the channel, even they admit that strong public access programming can draw an additional clientele to the tube and thus enhance revenues. "I don't see the two as incompatible at all," says Brian Sullivan, a local manager for Group W Cable. "Good public access can draw additional viewers."

In broadcasting, there is already a strong access tradition, although it can be said that it is not as effective as it ought to be. There is a right of reply to personal attack, which is part of a Fairness Doctrine that permits individual and institutional response to broadcast editorials and news coverage as well as a right to equal time in political broadcasts. There is also a tradition of ascertainment whereby attitudes of community leaders are sought out. These opportunities for access do not, at present, affect a large percentage of the population, but they could be used more judiciously by the access movement people.

Two other mechanisms for access are public opinion polls and two-way television made possible in some cable systems. Polls, if conducted properly, give all citizens an equal possibility of being chosen to have their views aired. Of course, the chance is quite small since sample sizes for national polls are tiny. A better job needs to be done in polling questions that truly concern the American people rather than those of interest solely to political figures and educators. Alex Edelstein of the University of Washington has been a leader in calling for public opinion studies that emphasize "salience information," that is, information of direct concern to people as ascertained in open-ended personal interviews. This, he says, is superior to having individual citizens rank the five most important issues in the country based on some preconceived list developed by elitist pollsters in their offices.

In Columbus, Ohio, in the 1970s an experiment was initiated with two-way cable television, called QUBE. It allowed for "instant in-home polls" and for people to "talk back" to the television set by voting on a variety of program choices, local issues, and social questions. Although QUBE has notable problems and is not yet at a Nirvana stage, it is another possible mechanism for citizen access to communication. Broadcast laws could also be studied closely for additional mandatory access provisions, although in the climate of deregulation in the 1980s this hope might be unrealistic.

Attempts to force the print media to provide greater public access will no doubt be thwarted by political forces at the legislative level and by the courts, where the judiciary is wary of prior restraints or special requirements for the press. Still, as the press continues to ask for more and more special privileges based on its social role of "representing the people," imaginative citizens and lawyers will probably look for an opening. (This is, in fact, one of the reasons why I have said earlier that it is dangerous for the press to ask for rights that the rest of us do not have.)

Providing a public right of access does not mean a perfect situation where people will be happy and satisfied all the time. It is not feasible to give every citizen in the population air time on television or a guest column in the newspaper. Thus, it may be necessary for the media to try to select representative views and citizens to stand in for the rest of us who cannot be heard. This selection is already done to a limited degree with letters to the editor.

Naturally, no one is required to listen to anyone else's views and in many instances getting a listener, whether in print or electronic media, will require the speaker to make compelling and persuasive presentations. We live in a real world and while communication might become an inherent human right, individual voices will need to live within realistic limits. There is nothing inconsistent about this limitation, though. To argue that the right of access might be limited to time, place, and circumstances or offered up to the channel capacity of available resources does not diminish its importance. After all, freedom of the press itself lives with many constraints and barriers. It is not in full flower at every moment, nor need it be to exist.

Professor Barron has done us a favor by making his case in law review articles and in the courts. Just because he did not prevail in a rather weak case is no reason to doubt that access would benefit individuals and society in many ways. Ayn Rand can have her "virtue of selfishness." Selfishness and greed are not the basis for a coherent and successful society although such a society can tolerate within limits these essentially negative forces. Nor am I persuaded by "red-baiting" references to a "people's press" in the Soviet Union or China. No one in the access movement is suggesting that the people take over the traditional media, wresting control from professional editors and managers. Instead, they are asking for a chance to be heard, to contribute to the community and national dialogue, to be represented in the media that claim to represent them and to act as public trustees. The question is one of truly participative media wherein all of us have some chance, however small, of being heard.

FURTHER READING

Barron, Jerome A. "Access to the Press: A New Concept of the First Amendment," *Seminar* (March 1969), 23–26.

_____. *Freedom of the Press for Whom? The Right of Access to Mass Media* (Bloomington: University of Indiana Press, 1973).

Cranberg, Gilbert. "Public Participation in the Press: New Look at the First Amendment," *Saturday Review* (Sept. 14, 1968), 136–38.

Dennis, Everette E. "The Press and the Public Interest: A Definitional Dilemma," *DePaul Law Review* 23 (Spring 1974), 937–960.

Gross, Gerald, ed. *The Responsibility of the Press* (New York: Simon and Schuster, Clarion Books, 1971).

Hocking, William Ernest. *Freedom of the Press: A Framework of Principle.* A report from The Commission on Freedom of the Press (Chicago: University of Chicago Press, 1947).

Murray, Edward. "The Editor's Right to Decide," *Seminar* (March 1970), 23–26.

Rand, Ann. *Virtue of Selfishness* (New York: New American Library, 1964).

Rubin, Bernard. *Media, Politics, and Democracy* (New York: Oxford University Press, 1977). See especially Chapter 4—"Popular Participation and Media."

_____. *Small Voices and Great Trumpets, Minorities and the Media* (New York: Praeger, 1980).

Schmidt, Benno C., Jr. *Freedom of the Press V. Public Access* (Springfield, Mass.: Praeger Publishers, Inc., 1976).

Wicklein, John. *Electronic Nightmare: The New Communications and Freedom* (New York: Viking Press, 1981).

Media
Pluralism

5

The value of media pluralism stems from the idea that democracy is best served by diversity in the communication market place, that a variety of competing voices can provide the public with a multiplicity of information and opinions on which to base its decisions. The long-standing trend toward the concentration of ownership in the mass media (chains buying chains, fewer and fewer owners) as well as the declining number of competing newspapers and broadcast outlets in many cities suggests that media pluralism is declining. Further, arguments about the homogenization of media content due to market research, rating services, and other measures suggest that diversity in content and overall pluralism are also down. Media pluralism, then, is usually ascertained by considering the actual number of publications and broadcast outlets in the market place, the nature of the ownership of those outlets, and finally, the characteristics of the content (programming and news) they deliver. Clearly, the prevailing view is that diversity and pluralism are down, regardless of whether one justifies and supports the reasons this has happened.

Dennis: Media pluralism is *not* shrinking.

The response is predictable. A newspaper dies and editorialists throughout the nation declare that "a voice is lost and we are poorer for it." The early 1980s were devastating years for large afternoon daily newspapers (called PMs) as the *Philadelphia Bulletin, Cleveland Press, Washington Star, Minneapolis Star, Des Moines Tribune,* and *Oregon Journal* either died or were merged into larger, healthier morning dailies. It was a blow for diversity, a blow for media pluralism. Or was it?

The purpose of this discussion is to move beyond the usual knee-jerk reaction to the condition of "our declining dailies" and to get a more substantive understanding of media pluralism. To do that we have to get some things straight.

Debating about media pluralism requires a close look at one of the most curious and complex concepts in the field of mass communication. It is a strange mixture of constitutional history, economic theory, sociology, and good old-fashioned moralizing. To begin with, few would doubt that one of the intentions of the press freedom clause of the First Amendment was to allow for diversity of information and opinion. This diversity was to protect citizens from governmental control of information and ideas. Today we can add to this concern the fear many critics have of the private sector, which owns our communication system and which has profit, not pluralism, as its primary motivating force. In addition to the component of diversity of information and opinion, media pluralism also involves the existence of different ethnic and cultural subgroups in the population. A central assumption here is that no single subgroup should dominate the others.

When reduced to its fundamental features, media pluralism usually means two things: diversity of ownership and diversity of content in the communications available to the public. The two are thought to be interrelated. At one level it would seem that the question of whether media pluralism is expanding or shrinking requires only a simple empirical response. Can't we simply count the number of media organizations in society, see who owns them, and have an answer? The answer is "No, not exactly," for the problem is more complex and difficult to sort out because the number of voices is only a part of the equation. It's what's in them that counts and there is no easy, universally accepted way to measure diversity of content. The problem is even more clouded because deep-seated values, prevailing prejudices, and excessive moralizing engulf the notion of media diversity and pluralism.

For these reasons media pluralism is rarely the subject of rational debate. Critics snarl, growl, and carp. They use economic forecasts and other quantitative data as they see fit. Some of them think newspapers and other media outlets are mainly public service organizations, rather than economic entities. To them chain owners and other media managers are self-serving and essentially evil individuals who would package and sell off our democratic values if they could, to make a profit. Indeed, former *New York Times* reporter Molly Ivins once picked up on this with a bit of black humor when she told a convention of newspaper owners, "I thought you people would be a bunch of egg-sucking child molesters."

Just when the issue of media pluralism emerged is not clear, but by the 1920s critics like Oswald Garrison Villard of *The Nation* were decrying the growing economic concentration of the newspaper industry. Chain ownership, Villard and others believed, had unfortunate social consequences and would lessen chances for the Miltonian ideal wherein truth and falsehood could grapple in the market place of ideas. The fewer the voices, the less variety of information and opinion.

As newspaper chains became dominant and as fewer American cities had competing dailies (a trend that continues today), it was natural that critics would conclude that diversity was down and pluralism was threatened. This rather predictable reaction meshes nicely with two well-embedded American values, namely, that (1) *bigness is bad* and (2) *localism is desirable*. As media researcher Ben Compaine explains,

> Control of information, news, and ideas should be spread around as much as possible. Locally owned newspapers and broadcast stations, many book publishers, scores of independent film producers and distributors would supposedly provide greater access to diverse opinions than fewer owners controlling an identical number of media outlets. (Compaine, 1981).

No wonder that publisher Frank Muncey, who was known for his cold-hearted business values, raised hackles when he wrote in 1908 that "there is no business that cries so loud for organization and combination as that of newspaper publishing."

Many commentators who are concerned about media concentration and what they think is a decline in media pluralism look at only one variable: the number of newspaper owners. This coupled with the overall decline in the number of newspapers alarms them. Less often do they consider whether group or chain ownership increases or decreases diversity of media content in a given community. Some newspaper chains like Knight-Ridder have a reputation for quality. Their papers are well-edited and have a wide range of columnists and feature material that leave their readers with considerably more variety than some weaker independently owned newspapers. In this instance, strong ownership has real social benefits. Of course, there are also group owners like Thomson and Newhouse that do not have a reputation for quality. I have personally watched two cities (St. Cloud, Minn., and Salem Ore.) where most knowledgeable observers agree that the Gannett Company's purchase of local newspapers resulted in a strengthened editorial product.

In fairness, though, I will concede that studies of the consequences of chain ownership and concentration paint a mixed portrait of their actual effect on quality and diversity. Generally, though, I believe that the scales tilt slightly toward advantages that come from chain ownership especially with regard to editorial sources such as news services, columns, comics, etc. The record of chain newspapers with regard to editorial page offerings (as seen in endorsements for Presidential candidates) is less impressive. Chain papers, studies show, are more likely to make endorsements than are independent newspapers, but also more likely to endorse the same candidate. There are exceptions, of course, but I would rate the issue here as something of a draw. While independent newspapers, according to a national study with which I was associated, seemed to avoid controversy and thus cheat their readers out of the "diverse local voice" they might expect, the chains seemed to stamp out their presidential endorsement editorials with the same cookie cutter.

If we stopped our inquiry at the newspaper doorstep, I would be hard pressed to make my case for increased pluralism. However, the media world includes much more than newspapers. In fact, fewer and fewer Americans subscribe to or read a daily newspaper and it is obvious that the newspapers play a less important role in our national life than they once did.

What of other media outlets? Do they contribute to diversity and pluralism or not? First, in broadcasting there are several thousand stations and no one can own more than seven A.M., seven F.M., and, seven TV stations, thus preventing monopoly control. Broadcast news programming has increased markedly in recent years as local radio and television stations compete in the rating for supremacy in news as well as entertainment programming. However, broadcast editorializing is still rather sparse and hardly a major source of guidance to the public.

The magazine field is a great source of diversity of ownership and content. While there is some group ownership, the magazine industry has less concentration of ownership than other American industries, including newspapers, and the possibility for new magazines to develop is very great indeed. Although they were the first mass medium in America, magazines no longer court the mass audience to the extent that they once did, but rather try for a quite defined, specialized leadership. They want the skiier, for example, not a mythical average citizen. This means that the range and diversity of content in magazines is almost limitless, with nearly every possible special interest represented. Magazines also carry a wide variety of opinion ranging from the far left to the far right; some are downright anarchistic. There are critics who argue that this diversity is meaningless because many magazines have relatively small circulations and are therefore not reaching enough people to make a difference. This objection is largely nonsense because a small, respected journal can have enormous impact. A specialized publication like the *New England Journal of Medicine,* which enjoys enormous respect in the medical community, can easily have more influence and impact than a network television show on the same subject by the sheer force of that publication's authoritativeness with an audience that counts.

The field of book publishing is another area where diversity of information and opinion is at a premium. While publishers have been more attuned to a marketing approach in recent years and are not likely to publish works without any profit potential, they are still offering thousands of new voices in the market place every year. One only need prowl local bookstores to see the incredible range of ideas that are put behind the covers of books. Like magazines, most individual books have a fairly narrow audience and tend to be specialized, but those with revolutionary or startling new ideas are quickly picked up and disseminated by other media.

Finally, the rapidly expanding field of cable communication and other new technologies, such as direct broadcast service, have large promise for diversity and pluralism both because of their varied general offerings and also because of those programs calibrated to specific ethnic groups, subcultures, and interests. In many cities now there are at least 12 available channels, while many others have more than 30 and some will soon have 100 or more. Remember that each channel can be multiplied by the 24 hours in the day which makes the potential for diverse programs quite massive. Just under 30 percent of the nation is "wired," that is, hooked up to cable service, and this percentage should climb to more than 50 percent in about five years. Cable programmers offer hundreds of possibilities in special programming for women, the aged, ethnic minorities, children, and others. There are specialized sports networks, another that covers Congress, even outlets for soft-porn and much, much more. There are news services offered by Associated Press, Dow Jones, UPI, and Reuters. Ted Turner's Cable News Network was so successful that it has spawned other 24-hour cable news competition such as Group W. Before long most cities will also have cable public access channels that will allow local citizens and groups to make their own television programs and present their viewpoints as an alternative to the traditional media fare of the commercial programmers.

All this adds up to a portrait of media diversity both of ownership and of a content that would blow a circuit in the brains of the Framers who worried about keeping newspapers free from governmental licensing and control. In a society where points of view range from serious commentary about foreign affairs to proposals for more nude beaches, there is clearly a good deal of diversity. Even ethnic and cultural subgroups benefit from the communication revolution of the 1980s—both in the traditional media, which are seeking minority audiences, and in new media which are developing programs tailor-made for Blacks, Chicanos, Native Americans, and others.

If we once had reason to worry that national networks and conglomerate control of local newspapers and broadcast stations might lead to a nation of homogenized interests, the electronic revolution, especially as represented by cable, ought to relieve many fears. Naturally, some large firms have moved into this business (Time Inc., for example, owns Home Box Office and Cinemax), but there are still many alternative voices.

The diverse sources of information and opinion are almost mind boggling. These are with us already in greater numbers than any of us can hope to comprehend, let alone use. The real secret of intellectual survival for the consumer in an information society with these massive offerings lies in understanding the range of possibilities and knowing how to use them to personal advantage. There are, of course, reasons to be concerned about information-rich people vs. information-poor people. Information is power and some information will no doubt be priced so high that it will be out of reach of many people. Even then, though, through the prudent use of libraries and other public sources, most of us will have such enormous choices, so rich and varied, that anyone who suggests that media pluralism is diminishing will look quite silly. Diversity of ownership and content are up, not down.

Merrill: Media pluralism *is* shrinking.

As it is with many controversial journalistic topics, the root of discord connected with the issue of media pluralism lies in a failure to be specific as to the terms of argument. This, I think, is especially true in a discussion of media pluralism.

The topic before us is whether or not media pluralism is growing or shrinking. Professor Dennis has made a reasonable case, using media as diverse as daily newspapers and books, that overall pluralism in the United States is growing instead of shrinking. And, when we look at all the specialized publications, tape decks, records, cable television programs, and other broadcast outlets now available to the consumer, we must agree that—in this sense at least—pluralism is expanding.

But, actually, when most journalists talk about the shrinkage of pluralism and the danger of increasing group ownership, they are not talking about *total* media (nonjournalistic) pluralism. Rather they are concerned about the shrinkage of *news* media.

Journalists are talking about newspapers being brought out by groups (like Gannett), about dailies (like the *Washington Star*) that are disappearing from the scene, and about one-newspaper cities which restrict the news/commentary options of the citizenry. In effect, they are referring to a *journalistic* restriction of pluralism or diversity, not to a shrinkage of pluralism in the total communications system of the whole country.

It is true that the totality of voices in the United States is growing. I have no agrument on this. We are bombarded on all sides with a constant barrage of communications, pouring in on us from multiplying sources. But this is not the kind of pluralism journalists (and I) are concerned about. We are talking about newspapers, newsmagazines, and other primarily journalistic media. The names of Newhouse, Gannett, Scripps, Hearst, Knight-Ridder, and Thomson today roll off the tongue more readily than the names of individual newspapers; editors have become anonymous as have publishers—unless they are the names of the big group owners.

I shall not argue *quality*. It is possible that a group-owned newspaper is better, as is often contended, than an independent one. But it also may be worse. Quality, I think, depends on the personnel involved at a particular time on a particular newspaper. What I am talking about is quantity of journalistic media. There seems no doubt among people who keep up with such things that the number of newspapers is decreasing. In addition, the number of group-owned newspapers is increasing as is the number of single-newspaper cities. All this points to quantitative shrinkage of pluralism.

By the late 1970s, for example, fewer than 4 percent of the nation's cities had competing newspapers. More than half of the nation's dailies (more than two-thirds of the daily circulation) were owned by groups. In the early 1980s almost 1,100 dailies were owned by groups (more than 60 percent of all dailies). The number of newspaper groups stood at 170, and group-owned papers accounted for nearly three fourths of the total U.S. circulation.

It is quite true, and I have made a point of this myself (in *Media, Messages, and Men*), that there are different kinds of pluralism to be considered. And, besides, there are "levels" of pluralism which cannot be ignored. Unfortunately, most discussants talk only of pluralism in a monolithic way—usually meaning the number of separate media units. And many people go further and limit pluralism to the number of *independently owned* media units.

But there is at least one other important type of pluralism.

Message pluralism must be considered. It is quite clear that message pluralism is very important and that there can be a greater diversity of messages even in one newspaper than there could be in several newspapers. Therefore, there need not be a positive correlation between the number of newspapers and the number of messages. However, it is usually assumed that this is the case.

Besides the types of pluralism mentioned, there are distinct "levels" of pluralism which must be taken into consideration. There is *system* pluralism, the level which is being referred to when someone talks about how much diversification there is in our media or press system. The total news system is what is being considered. Then, there is the *community* level of pluralism. This level gets the concept of pluralism closer to home. The question of importance here is: How much diversity is present at the *local* level? To many persons system pluralism is really unimportant compared with community pluralism.

Obviously there could be other types and levels of diversity or pluralism. But these are the important ones which must be considered when one is discussing or debating the topic of press or media pluralism.

It may well be that, thinking of the topic in terms of "system pluralism," Professor Dennis is right: pluralism is indeed growing, not shrinking. But thinking about pluralism in terms of local or community pluralism (the really important level, in my opinion), I must maintain that pluralism or diversity is shrinking. How does it really affect *me* here in my locality that *throughout the whole country* pluralism may be expanding. The diversity that I want is here and now (in *my* news media), not what might be available in Oregon, Maine, Florida, Texas, or Washington, D.C.

It may well be also that, thinking about "message pluralism," Professor Dennis is right again: the number and variety of individual messages is indeed growing, not shrinking—especially on the *system* level. But how many people read more than one newspaper or watch more than one network newscast at a time? A good case can be made that potential pluralism is not what is important, that what matters is the actual, pragmatic pluralism—the diversity of messages that gets to the individual audience member.

In view of what I have just said about pluralism and its types and levels, I am left in the strange position of debating a "ghost topic." If we are talking about diversity of ownership media, then I think I am safe in saying that pluralism is shrinking in the United States. If we are talking about diversity or pluralism as it relates to total number of units or media, then I think Professor Dennis is correct in saying that pluralism is growing. And, even if we are talking about diversity of substantive items or viewpoints, I would suspect that Professor Dennis is correct. Truthfully, I can't say as to this last type of pluralism because it would take detailed, thorough, and continuing content analysis to prove anything about this item/viewpoint diversity. Nobody has shown any willingness to tackle such a study, so the issue must remain unresolved—at least for now.

When Professor Dennis and those who agree with him say that press pluralism is growing, I cannot really disagree with them for I do not know exactly what types and levels they are referring to. But neither can I agree with them.

This whole subject is one which demands precise definitions, in the first place, and systematic research and analysis in the second place. So far neither has surfaced in American journalism. Therefore, it is my belief that the jury must remain out on this question. At present it cannot be determined whether pluralism is growing or contracting.

And beyond this, there is really no way to get into the *evaluative* aspects of this question, given the current state of research. What I mean is this: It may well be that fewer media can (or do) provide a greater variety of information and viewpoints. This would go against the conventional wisdom, but it might well be the case. Some people contend that *fewer is better;* they may be right. We don't really know, and so far as I am aware, there is no real attempt to get at such questions.

For that matter, we normally assume that more information or viewpoints are better than less information and fewer viewpoints. This is nothing more than an assumption, but it is one which we use as a basis for many of our concerns about media or press pluralism. We usually assume that pluralism, in any of its forms, is good. The more information and the greater variety of information we are exposed to the better the situation is. Normally we do not take other factors into consideration—factors such as the truth or falsity of the information, differences in validity and sophistication of the viewpoints expressed, or the superficiality or thoroughness of the messages presented. All these factors are vitally important, of course, and they must be tackled by any person seriously concerned with the subject of journalistic diversity or pluralism.

FURTHER READING

Bagdikian, Ben H. "Newspaper Mergers in the Final Phase," *Columbia Journalism Review* (March–April 1977), 17–22.

_____. "Conglomeration Concentration and the Media," *Journal of Communication* (Spring 1980, 59–60).

Botein, Michael. *Legal Restrictions on Ownership of the Mass Media* (New York: Advanced Media Publishing Associates, 1977).

Compaine, Benjamin M. *Who Owns the Media? Concentration of Ownership in the Mass Communications Industry* (New York: Harmony Books, 1979).

Gitlin, Todd. "The New Technology: Pluralism or Banalty," *Democracy,* 4 (Oct. 1981), *1*, 60–76.

McCombs, Maxwell E. "Mass Media and the Marketplace," *Journalism Monographs,* No. 24 (Lexington, Ky.: Assn. for Education in Journalism, 1972).

Merrill, J. C., and Ralph L. Lowenstein. *Media, Messages, and Men* (New York: Longman, 1979).

Owen, Bruce M. *Economics and Freedom of Expression* (Cambridge, Mass.: Ballinger Books, 1975).

Rucker, Bryce W. *The First Freedom* (Carbondale, Ill.: Southern Illinois University Press, 1966).

Sterling, Christopher H., and Timothy R. Height. *The Mass Media: Aspen Institute Guide to Communication Industry Trends* (New York: Praeger, 1978).

Power of
the Media

6

Whether and to what degree the mass media have power has been widely debated. For many years the concept of the "power of the press" was a given, documented by historians, propaganda researchers, and others. That the press and later other media could move minds and goad people to action was widely believed. However, in the 1940s in study after study, this popular public view was severely challenged by empirical evidence. A more modest view of the power of the press evolved, and especially in the scholarly community a theory of "minimal effects" of mass communication has been in vogue. The press and other media, this view goes, mainly have the power to reinforce what people already believe, the power not to move the public mind but to influence some opinion leaders. Other forces such as the family, social groups, religious beliefs, and political parties have greater impact on the individual than do the mass media. Texts in psychology, political science, sociology, and other fields clearly downplayed the power of the press, saying that media operate in a nexus with other factors. The jury is still out on this question of press or media power and, in one form or another, the issue continues to be debated.

Dennis: The media *are* quite powerful.

Anyone who lives in the modern world and has a modicum of common sense will agree immediately with this statement. So why debate it? The reason is that for years new journalism and communication students have been cautioned about overestimating the impact and influence of the mass media. The conclusion was that the media were not really very powerful after all. Now something is changing.

The publication in 1981 of Volume 32 of the *Annual Review of Psychology* occurred without notice in the press and with less than a resounding ripple among media scholars in the United States. Yet, one chapter had a message of profound importance for media professionals and students of mass communications. In measured language, researchers Donald Roberts and Christine Bachen wrote, "the past decade . . . has witnessed a revival of the view that the mass media exert powerful influences on the way people perceive, think about, and ultimately act in their world" (pp. 307–308).

To some this may not seem such a startling statement. We are rarely without graphic examples of the alleged power of the media whether it is in foreign policy (where government leaders sometimes play to the media), in national politics (where some critics claim that television has taken over the role once played by political parties), or in social behavior (where we worry whether sexually suggestive advertisements for designer jeans are corrupting the values of youth). Concern about the media clearly extends beyond the halls of academe and into everyday life as terms like "media event," "hype," and "image" become commonplace in our language.

The media have been replete with examples like these for many years. Quite naturally this emphasis has led to the popular conception that media institutions have influence, impact, power, and, yes, effects. While it is true that these terms were never defined to everyone's satisfaction, there has long been a shared notion that mass media institutions shape our thinking, influence our attitudes and opinions, and contribute toward particular behavior such as voting and buying certain goods.

Mass communication was an invention of the nineteenth century, but did not attract much scholarly attention until after World War I. From that time until the mid 1940s, the yield of scholarly studies contributed to the conclusion that the media had enormous power.

74

During this period, the scholarly view and the lay view were virtually congruent. Of course, there was not universal agreement about just what the media could and could not do. There were shadings of differences in interpretation and approach depending on whether one was listening to a critic, an empirical social scientist, a media practitioner, or the uninitiated lay person. Still, at the most simple, basic level there was considerable agreement with a hypodermic needle model of media effects wherein the media infected the minds of individuals directly with powerful messages. This was the concept of the powerful press.

This shared perspective would change under the scholarly and professional leadership of sociologist Paul Lazarsfeld and a generation of empirical researchers. By trying to isolate questions that could be probed by social researchers, Lazarsfeld and company narrowed the focus of the media effects discussion to *provable impact* as demonstrated by specific, short-term studies. Looking mainly at attitude and opinion change in electoral campaigns, these researchers brought us the two-step flow and a model of personal influence wherein mass communication was not necessarily a central and dominant force, but instead one that operated in conjunction with interpersonal communication and various socializing influences. When empirical researchers were asked to explain media power, they used vague qualifying language and said they thought the earlier view of a powerful press was probably wrong. Thus came the idea of minimal effects of mass communication. This view, prominent among social scientists, had a strange and fragmenting influence on scholars' perceptions of mass communication. At the same time, the public's view of media power did not change. Even in instances when one might have doubted the power of the press to change voting behavior, for example, plausible common-sense explanations were found. When it became evident that newspaper editorial endorsements for Presidential candidates did not have a direct effect on the voting public, people often chose to believe that this fact did not really challenge media power. After all, we were told, reporters are liberals and their favorable treatment of liberal candidates drowns out stuffy, conservative endorsements on the editorial page.

The notion that the media had little direct influence on people led to much confusion and outright disbelief in the research and researchers. This disbelief fostered antiintellectualism and a deep chasm between practitioners and scholars, especially in journalism education where students got mixed messages. Students got a minimal effects indoctrination in their mass media classes and also in economics, political science, sociology, and history. Teachers in their desire to simplify and explain too often presented the great researchers as purist scholars who sneered at any notion of major or powerful media effects. Rarely did they suggest that thoughtful people using different assumptions and different methods might come to quite different conclusions. No wonder students found themselves in a conceptual muddle. Think, for example, of the journalism student who is told by a public opinion teacher that the media have minimal effects only to discover that the reporting teacher thinks newspaper stories can have powerful consequences. Then, in the everyday world, the student watches television and perceives quite rightly that advertisers certainly act as though media can move goods by encouraging people to buy them.

While it is difficult to doubt the scholarly benefits that came with the minimal effects perspective, it did tend to fragment our understanding of mass communication and appeared to set practitioners against researchers. Contrasting the powerful effects approach with the minimal effects view does provide useful background for the continuing debate over media effects, especially now when people are arguing for a return to the concept of powerful media with some modification.

One of the main reasons we study and debate media effects is to get a handle on our own thinking, to trace our own intellectual history and chart increments and obstacles in its development.

Whether the dramatic shifts in research findings (as noted by Roberts and Bachen) truly represent what the historian of science Thomas Kuhn would call paradigm change or complete change in our thought process is not clear, but scholars increasingly think this might be so.

The first stirrings of the apparent shift in communication research came not in a new and startling book or theory, but in the shared views of a number of scholars, some of whom were well-established while others were just beginning their careers. The distinguished researcher Wilbur Schramm urged study of the "quiet, continuing effects" of mass communication which, he said, were largely ignored and might yield important findings. Melvin DeFleur, author of the *Theories of Mass Communication,* said we should explore the role of mass communication in the enlargement of peoples' belief systems which he thought might seriously challenge the narrow, limited conclusions of earlier studies. The German researcher Elisabeth Noelle-Neumann, called for a return to a belief in the concept of a powerful mass media. "The fact is," she wrote, "the decisive factors of mass media are not brought to bear in the traditional laboratory experiment" (Noelle-Newmann, 1973, p. 67). Adding to the discussion, Peter Clarke and F. Gerald Kline asserted that What people learn from communication activity is a more rewarding topic for media effects research than attitude formation or change. Offering a striking observation in his studies of media bias in electoral campaigns, John P. Robinson wrote that evidence now exists that under certain conditions, the media can have political impact. Robinson was one of the first to seriously challenge the minimal effects perspective, asking rhetorically in a *Journalism Quarterly* article, "Can the Media Affect Behavior After All?" The agenda-setting studies of Maxwell McCombs and Donald Shaw concluded that the informational/learning role of the media was its most important effect. This meant that the media would tell people not what to *think* but what to *think about*. The scholars mentioned above were quite careful and understated in their new view of media power, but others were not so quiet. Sociologist Todd Gitlin denounced the Lazarsfeld (minimal effects) tradition in an article that accused researchers of failing to "put the crucial questions" because of "intellectual, ideological and institutional commitments" (Gitlin, 1978, p. 205). Said Gitlin, "behind the idea of the relative unimportance of the mass media lies a skewed, faulty concept of importance, similar to the faulty concept of power" (Gitlin, 1978 p. 205). To Gitlin, this had the effect of justifying the existing system of media ownership, control, and purpose:

> By its methodology, media sociology has highlighted the recalcitrance of audiences, their resistance to media-generated message, and not their dependency, their acquiescence, their gullibility. It has looked to "effects" of broadcast programming in specifically behaviorist fashion defining "effects" so narrowly, microscopically, and directly as to make it very likely that survey studies could only show slight "effects" at most. It has enshrined short run effects as "measures" of "importance" largely because these "effects" are measurable in a strict, replicable, behavioral sense, thereby deflecting attention of larger social meanings of mass media production (Gitlin, 1978, pp. 203–206).

This view comes mainly from humanistic reasoning and observation. However, Roberts and Bachen reached a similar conclusion based on a review of several areas of research, including patterns of media use, probes of children, and media studies of uses and gratifications, information transmission and processing, the knowledge gap hypothesis, the cultivation of beliefs, attention and comprehension, responses to advertising, political socialization, antisocial behavior, prosocial effects, and sex role socialization. This research raises new questions and expands the arena for investigation well beyond the old targets into the largely uncharted realm of cognitive effects. It is here that many studies, with striking and distinctive findings, are encouraging researchers to reconsider a modification of the minimal effects doctrine. Several recent texts about media effects also make this point. It is not surprising that one of the most articulate proponents of a new view, the German researcher Noelle-Neumann, says there are clues in research that haven't been considered much before. They are

1. *Ubiquity of the media*—the ability to be everywhere, to dominate the information environment. The media are so ubiquitous at times that it is difficult to escape a message.

2. *Cumulation of messages*—one should look beyond the individual, fragmented messages to the cumulative effect over time. There is frequent repetition of the message that tends to reinforce its impact.

3. *Consonance of journalists*—there is remarkable agreement and demographic similarity among journalists and other media professionals. This leads to a sameness in newspapers and newscasts and limits the options the public has for selective perception (Noelle-Neumann, 1974, paraphrased from pp. 67–112).

Similarly, communication researcher James Lemert attacks what he calls the "simple reductionist model" of the minimal effects school which measured media influence mainly through attitude change. Lemert would have us discard the idea that attitude change is either necessary or sufficient for public opinion change. He believes that minimal effects researchers attempted to explain society with limited information about individuals. The mass media, he says, can have a powerful impact on the information given to decision makers. By integrating research on public opinion with the role of decision makers and journalists, Lemert proposes studies that would take effects research beyond "simple reductionism." Importantly, he recognizes that we must first understand the prevailing research patterns in order to use their strengths and avoid their limitations. Like Noelle-Neumann and others, he is concerned with the news media as collectors of attitude information and with the context of attitude information and change.

When the dust is settled on the present media effects debate, I believe that a true paradigm shift will be evident. We have, in fact, seen an integration of all the stages of change that accompany paradigm change. There has been incremental change as represented in the empirical scholarship wherein researchers are framing new questions that take them into cognitive areas and beyond the limitations of short-run effects studies. This change has come about by a useful collaboration of the people interested in the largely externally oriented social impact with those who care more about individuals and their attitudes as well as those who care about media organizations. In the early stages of some of this research, findings that conflicted with prevailing patterns and widely held beliefs were often seen as change by exception. Eventually, as these findings recurred, they replaced the earlier view. Some scholars say there has been a pendulum shift and they would decry the "errors of the past" by putting a figurative stake through poor Lazarsfeld's heart. If research really does tell us that we need a new view of media power it may be due to studies that probe such issues as the social construction of reality and long-term cumulative effects. Notably, research of this kind is no longer confined to a small group of theoretical researchers in mass communication or social psychology and related fields. Persons from within mass communication with interests in history, law, institutional analysis, economics, and other topics are also working diligently on questions often central to media impact, influence, and effect. Even these terms are getting greater clarification and more precise definition as scholars raise new questions and try to make more refined calibrations.

All of these things will help us understand the impact and influence of mass communication with greater care and sophistication than ever before. We will not return to the point of having uncritical awe of so-called media power, but we will understand better how mass communication works in the context of other social forces without underestimating its importance and influence. Clearly, the media are powerful.

Merrill: The media are *not* so powerful.

The first sentence of the preceding "challenge" puts me in a difficult position. Since I live in the modern world and think I have at least a "modicum of common sense," I find that I must agree immediately with the contention that the media are powerful. And yet, I am supposed to be saying here that they are not powerful.

But, as Professor Dennis says in the remainder of his first paragraph, there have been researchers who have maintained that the impact and influence of the media have been overstated. So the topic is, in spite of its fuzzy nature, still controversial.

However, I am put in a difficult position by the very wording of this proposition. I really cannot maintain that the media have *no* power and that their impact is *nonexistent*. It is all too obvious that media have some power and that their influence on society cannot be denied. Advertisers, pragmatists and realists that they are, recognize the power of the media. Sociologists have documented various trends started and maintained by media attention. Politicians have contended that their careers have been helped or ruined by attention or neglect by the media. Panics have been precipitated by the media. Riots, demonstrations, skyjackings, and acts of terrorism are thought to be stimulated by media publicity. The "contagion" aspect of events is obviously connected with public exposure.

I cannot, and will not, deny that the media have *some* power. But the question really is: Do we know for certain that the media are *in themselves* powerful? Or are they simply secondary factors, triggering mechanisms if you will, which have various impacts in society under certain circumstances?

Let us admit immediately that some media, under some conditions, with some people, have some effects or impact. Media, however, do not work in a vacuum. Certainly Paul Lazarsfeld and his colleagues were right when they concluded that the mass media operate in conjunction with many social forces to bring about certain results. The implication of much of this "effects" research is that mass communication is influential but not central or dominant in the model of personal influence.

A candidate for office, let us say, is elected. Did the media put him in? The answer must be, "No—but they probably played their part." The candidate appeared to many persons in person—as an individual without media help. He conversed; he debated; he answered questions. He used the telephone. He and his family and friends knocked on doors and handed out cards. He spoke at the Rotary Club and at the county fair. He was an individual as well as a media event.

In addition, we must recognize that the candidate *himself* (exclusive of the power, presumed or real, of the media) had talents, effectiveness, charisma, a friendly and trustworthy smile, and other personal attributes which made him popular and electable. The media themselves did not give him these attributes. The media may have served as channels whereby the public or portions of it were exposed to these attributes—but they were personal, not media-induced. How can researchers, seeking the impact of the media, separate personal "power" from media "power"? I do not think they can. Certainly there is no evidence, to my knowledge, that can show that all other impacting factors can be separated out—so the conclusion is that the media have no more than tangential or minimal impact.

Journalists, of course, like to think that they and their media have great power and that they are movers and shakers in society. It is satisfying to them to think that they are king-makers, agenda-setters, corruption-unearthers, society-improvers. Of course, they are not quite so sure of their power when someone points out that the negativism, violence, sensationalism, and sexploitation permeating the media might be having a deleterious effect on society. They seem to see themselves as having only "positive" power and seldom if ever "negative" power.

While there are many communications scholars today, such as DeFleur, Noelle-Neumann, Clarke, and Kline alluded to by Professor Dennis, who call for more research of media impact in the real (nonexperimental) world, hardly any research of this nature has been done. How does one get at the impact of the media when trying to study them in a total social symbiosis? How does one separate or isolate purely media effects from other effects? These questions have been addressed, of course, but have not been satisfactorily answered. When scholars like Max McCombs and Don Shaw conclude that agenda setting by the media is an important role and has "power" in that it tells people what to think *about,* they have stated an obvious informational principle, but they have come closer to specifying the real power of the media. Of course, I will generally think more about news events I read much about and see prominently on the TV screen than I will about those which are ignored or minimally treated by the media. Nobody can deny that. I may be aware of these events, or even think about them, because of their media attention, but the question still remains: What impact does such consciousness have on me?

A locked front door to a building may cause me to go around to a side door to enter. In one sense, then, the lock has power and has caused a change in my activity; it has modified my interaction with my environment. But how has it affected me? Studying the lock will not answer the question. Neither will a study of the quantitative aspects of my new and more elongated journey to another door. Only an in-depth psychological study will cast some light on the power or impact on me of the locked front door.

What I am trying to say, I guess, is that our lives are constantly affected or changed by a multitude of factors—some of which are messages reaching our brains—and these factors are so complex and intertwined as to defy clear determinations as to the impact of each. What we *think* obviously has some kind of effect on our lives. What we *do* is also important. But what we do is not always determined by what we think, so we cannot say that if we have certain information we will act in a certain way on the basis of that information—or, in fact, that we will act at all.

John P. Robinson has written that evidence now exists "that under certain conditions" media can have political impact. That is almost like saying that under certain conditions an Alpine valley town can be destroyed by an avalanche of snow. Of course, media *can* have political impact. I can just as well say that under certain conditions media can *not* have political impact.

Professor Dennis mentions James Lemert's attack on the "simple reductionist model" of minimal effects which measures media influence mainly through attitude change. Lemert says, according to Dennis, that the mass media can have a powerful impact on the information given to decision makers. I would go even further than that: I would say that the mass media can have *total* control and impact *on the information* given to the decision makers. (Impact on the *information:* Now here is a new concept!) At least this would certainly be true of the information given the decision makers by the media. Earlier I have maintained that people (including decision makers) get much information from sources other than the mass media.

What we seem to need in all this debating about media power are some clear definitions. I do not think most researchers and students in this area are really sure just what they are talking about. What do they mean by *power?* What is meant by *minimal effects?* Or *maximal effects?* What is meant by *media?* Just how *powerful* (by any definition) would the media need to be to be considered powerful or effective?

Are there not different types or forms of power? For instance, the providing of information (regardless of the impact) is one kind of power. Another kind of power would be the impact or effect of such information *on the mind.* Still another kind of power would be the impact or effect of such information *on the actions* of a person. Most often the distinctions among these kinds of power are ignored or minimized.

I would postulate that

1. Media are most powerful in furnishing information and setting agenda for members of a public.
2. Media are next most powerful in impinging on the thoughts, opinions, and attitudes of members of a public.
3. Media are least powerful in affecting actions of members of a public.

So, in conclusion, I will have to agree that media are powerful sometimes and to some extent. Just when they are and to what degree are questions crying out for more answers, more research. At present we know very little about media *power.* It may well be that media are really more powerful than media-power proponents think. But then, they may be far less powerful.

I cannot say in good conscience that media are not powerful, but I can, I think, say in good conscience that what power they have is shared with innumerable forces in society. I can also say that, so far as I am able to learn, media in themselves are not nearly as powerful (in any of the aspects of power) as journalists and other media people generally contend.

Babb, Laura L., ed. *Of the Press, by the Press, and Others, Too* (Boston: Houghton Mifflin, 1976).

Brucker, Herbert. *Communication is Power* (New York: Oxford University Press, 1973).

Comstock, George, et al. *Television and Human Behavior* (New York: Columbia University Press, 1978).

Daedalus. "Print Culture and Video Culture." A special issue. Vol. 111, No. 4, Fall 1982.

Davis, D. K., and S. J. Baran. *Mass Communication and Everyday Life: A Perspective on Theory and Effects* (Belmont, Ca: Wadsworth, 1981.

DeFleur, M. L., and Everette E. Dennis. *Understanding Mass Communication* (Boston: Houghton Mifflin, 1981).

Gitlin, Todd. "Media Sociology: The Dominant Paradigm." *Theory's Society* 6 (November 1978), 205–253.

———. *The Whole World is Watching* (Berkeley, University of California Press, 1980).

Jamison, Kathleen Hall, and Karlyn Kohrs Campbell. *The Interplay of Influence* (Belmont, Cal.: Wadsworth, 1983).

Klapper, Joseph T. *The Effects of Mass Communication* (New York: The Free Press, 1960).

Kraus, Sydney, and Dennis Davis. *The Effects of Mass Communication on Political Behavior* (University Park: Pennsylvania State University Press, 1976).

Lemert, James B. *Does Mass Communication Change Public Opinion After All?* (Chicago: Nelson-Hall, 1981).

McCombs, Maxwell, and Donald Shaw. "The Agenda-Setting Function of Mass Media," *Public Opinion Quarterly* 36 (1972), 176–187.

Mills, C. Wright. *Power, Politics, and People* (New York: Ballantine Books, 1962).

Noelle-Neumann, Elisabeth. "Return to the Concept of Powerful Mass Media." *Studies of Broadcasting* (1973), *9*, 67–112.

Reeves, Richard. "The Press's Great Threat," *Esquire* (August 1, 1978), 10, 13.

Roberts, D. F., and Christine M. Bachen. "Mass Communication Effects," *Annual Review of Psychology*, (February 1981), *32*, 307–356.

Rubin, Bernard. *Media, Politics, and Democracy* (New York: Oxford University Press, 1977). See especially Chapter 5—"Media and Election Trends."

Schramm, Wilbur, ed. *The Process and Effects of Mass Communication* (Urbana: University of Illinois Press, 1954).

Schramm, W., and William Porter. *Men, Women, Messages, and Media* (New York: Harper & Row, 1982).

Small, William J. *To Kill a Messenger: Television News and the Real World* (New York: Hastings House, 1970).

_____. *Political Power and the Press* (New York: Hastings House, 1972).

Stein, Robert. *Media Power: Who Is Shaping Your Picture of the World?* (Boston: Houghton Mifflin, 1972).

Quality
of Media Content

7

Critics of mass communication have hammered away for decades at the quality of media content. Whether one is discussing the information, opinion, or entertainment functions of the mass media, the quality of the fare offered to the public is often at issue. The standard view in communication history is that the press has gotten stronger, freer, and better over time. We have come to think of newspaper articles, movie scripts, and television scenarios as increasing in quality. To some, media content of two decades ago or earlier not only seems dated but of somewhat primitive quality compared with what is offered today. Others disagree. Criticism of media content usually focuses on (1) the substantive information or entertainment material being present as well as (2) the style or form of presentation. Especially in the first instance, there is strong support in scholarly commentary and criticism for the argument that media content is much improved. Often it is argued that audience preferences and tastes demand quality, and television programs, news content of newspapers, and magazines that do not meet this consumer-quality standard simply do not survive. This argument convinces some, but not others.

Dennis: Media content is generally of *poor* quality and getting worse.

Evaluating media content is a difficult task. If we have low expectations, almost anything goes and almost anything will seem better than it might have been. If we have high standards and measure what *is* against what *might be,* we are likely to be disappointed. Frankly, I come down in the middle. I look at today's media content against a standard of what is reasonable. And on that basis I am unimpressed by what I see in almost all of the individual mass media in the United States. True, there are rare pockets of quality in some of the so-called opinion and literary magazines and on public television, but for the most part the performance of the American media can only be termed a major embarrassment.

Questions of quality almost always are equated with matters of elitism vs. egalitarianism; it is assumed that quality is synonymous with a wealthy or highly educated audience which would make an intellectual assault on what the people really want. I would argue that this is not the case. I believe that the American people have too often been subjected to low-quality media content not because they want it, but because media professionals have an inaccurate understanding of public tastes.

The major motivating force for quality in the American media is little more than the *egos* of directors, producers, editors, broadcasters, and others. People who want to distinguish themselves from that which is commonplace have the motivation and interest to strive to do better by producing something that is distinctive. There is little reason beyond this to truly elevate the media and its content. These people are often thwarted by their industry's perception of what the market will bear.

What is it that distinguishes a quality performance by the media from one that is mediocre or poor? Contrary to the view of some egalitarian critics, appealing to rich or snobbish people is not the essential element, instead it is

1. *Beauty* as expressed in design, presentation, and format.
2. *Literary style* as expressed in writing either for print or electronic media.

3. *Universal appeal* in terms of those elements that touch the heart or mind and have a lasting impact.

4. *Impact* as seen in the long-term contribution of the material that is produced.

Finally, in my mind, an elevating influence is being able to say this is the best that can be done; it is better than that which has come before, and it can be clearly distinguished from earlier work, more primitive efforts, less informed approaches.

While I do not believe in the full-throttle theory of Excelsior (upward, onward ever), I do think there is a difference between stagnation and forward movement in media content.

Look at the newspaper, for example. Is today's newspaper better than the one that existed a few years or decades ago? By what measure do we answer this question? First I would look at the quality of writing. Is it more vital, more lively, more readable than that which appeared before? Next, I would consider the substantive information conveyed. Is it accurate? Is it complete? Is it compelling? Does it have proper context? I would also look at the methods reporters use in their work. Are these tools, whether in interviewing, use of documents and records, or corroboration of sources, an improvement over those used decades ago? If so, how and why? If not, why not? I would ask whether the newspaper is in touch with its audience. Does it resonate the concerns that people have? Does it understand its readers and calibrate material to their interests and needs?

When we address these questions squarely and well, the American newspaper is a quite deficient product. Few critics assert that the writing in the American press is sterling. Good writing is the exception, not the rule. Tom Winship, the gifted editor of the *Boston Globe*, has excoriated the American press for its lack of attention to writing:

> Newspapers are dying, in part, because they are dull and predictable. If we are going to attempt good writing we won't be able always to play it safe; we'll have to try new forms, new subjects, new voices, stories written and reported at new distances, stories that are shorter than usual and longer than usual. Some of them won't work for good writing is always experimental. (Winship, 1982, p. 22).

Experimental is the key word here. Most newspapers simply will not tolerate experimentation. They play it safe and what they produce results in what New Journalist Tom Wolfe calls a "paralyzing snoremonger" syndrome. Few critics think the writing in American newspapers is anything other than mediocre. The newspaper is not the home of America's best and most gifted prose. It could be. Literary giants of the past such as Hemingway, Faulkner, and others began their careers at newspapers and produced strong nonfiction prose that is memorable today. In 1982, when the brilliant sports writer Red Smith died, a number of publications produced samples of his writing. This work was notable mainly because it was so much unlike the turgid copy that usually appears on the modern sports page.

Writing, of course, is only one aspect of media performance. What of the methods, tools, and techniques of the journalist? Is there evidence that today's interviewing methods are significantly better than those of yesteryear? Are reporters more systematic, more meticulous, more competent in seeking out information for a wide variety of public records and documents? In spite of the surge toward investigative reporting in the early 1970s, it can rightly be said that today's reporters are guilty of journalistic primitivism. They are ignorant of their craft's history and frankly do not care about it. Take investigative reporting, for example. When Bob Woodward and Carl Bernstein did their Watergate investigation in the early 1970s, they were hailed as culture heroes. They were credited by some with bringing down a government and giving journalism a place at center stage again. But for journalism historians who compare this work with that of the great Muckrakers at the turn of the century, the Watergate boys and other modern investigative reporters do not measure up very well. By contrast, Lincoln Steffens, Ray Stannard Baker, and Ida Tarbell, the original Muckrakers, were world-class performers. Their prose was stronger; their investigative techniques about the same; the time they devoted to their projects, greater. After a close inspection of the performance of the 1980s investigative reporters and those of the early 1900s, I would have to give the nod to the folks at the turn of the century. This in itself is not particularly noteworthy, but it is sad that in eighty years, American journalism has progressed so little. If American medicine or science or even cooking methods had made as little progress, we would be terribly distressed, but we accept this sluggish performance by the media without much complaint. Indeed, the methods of a profession are often the best indicator of its progress.

One of the principal concerns of communicators is knowing and understanding the audience. Since the turn of the century there have been breathtaking advances in market and survey research and in other forms of audience analysis. Audiences can be examined for the intensity of readership and in other highly revealing ways. What does the average American newspaper know about its audience? The advertising department probably knows quite a bit, but little of this information filters down from the editors to reporters in the field. Reporters of the 1980s are probably more ignorant of their audience than their counterparts in the nineteenth century. In fact, there is evidence that the contemporary reporters are hopelessly out of touch with the reader because they tend to be part of an elite class. In a 1982 study three researchers at Michigan State University reported that "mobility, long working hours, and an attitude that news people are different from their readers contribute to journalists feeling out of touch." (Burgoon et. al., 1982, p. 5) This and other studies indicate that American journalists are not only insular, but are also quite contemptuous of their audience, referring to readers and viewers as "bozos" or "Joe Sixpak." (See Chapter 10.)

Now, you might ask, why should we expect today's reporters to be more knowledgeable or better informed? The answer is simple: research, computers, and techniques for examining the audience with real precision. I recall with much disappointment the results of a study I did with science editors on daily newspapers. They were an elite group of reporters and had a better grasp of research than almost any of their counterparts. Yet, when asked about the audience they were writing for their responses were incredibly unscientific as they confessed that they thought they were writing for "the Kansas City milkman." Many knowledgeable reporters genuinely thought they were writing for "everyone in the community" rather than the highly specific and defined audience which exists today. They were not making any practical use of the research data readily available to them as a tool to stay in touch with the reader or viewer.

What of commercial television content? Few would presume to argue that the soap operas which dominate daytime television are the best dramatic performances that we Americans are capable of producing and sustaining with advertising. Heavy-handed, melodramatic programs are the order of the day in the soaps that dominate daytime television. Evening programming is a little better, but not particularly noteworthy. In 1982 and 1983, when the networks announced that such highly regarded programs as "MASH," "Hill Street Blues," and "Lou Grant" were being dropped there was an almost universal lament that television's best quality was being diminished. Sometimes high quality programs that are dropped by the networks are picked up by cable, but by no means all. Naturally these cancellations act to discourage the development of similar quality fare.

Television is probably the best example of the "great leveler" theory of mass communication, which posits that one must appeal to a vast, homogeneous audience in order to succeed commercially. In the early 1960s, the chairman of the Federal Communications Commission declared that television was "a vast wasteland." Since then, not much has changed. Television programs are banal, silly, and of generally poor quality. Those that have higher quality usually are destined for the trash bin.

Television news is also worth examining. In recent years the most notable thing about TV news has been the addition of the news consultants who have had an enormous effect on program content. This addition has led not to more serious and thoughtful coverage of the public arena in a fashion that people will find interesting, but instead to "happy talk" news where newscasters reflect a kind of jovial idiocy as they make jokes between reports about plane crashes and bloody coups in foreign lands. There is more emphasis on the hair style of the anchorperson than the substance that person does or does not present on the evening news. There are certainly some pockets of good performance in television news as compared with radio news, which is still a headline service and an even vaster wasteland than television.

Not without considerable justification has television news been called "chewing gum for the eyes." It emphasizes trivial events that have a visual component regardless of their importance; it is biased toward the spectacle instead of the more subtle trend; it misleads the public by following the visual cue to the exclusion of deeper meaning.

Across much of the media, the economic glue that holds things together is advertising. And what of advertising? Is it of high quality? Does it elevate the American people? Do we admire it for its ethical sensitivity? For its fairness? For its devotion to truth? Of course not. These questions cannot even be put seriously. Advertising content is better than it was in the days of patent medicine shows and quacks, but it is hardly befitting a modern society. Advertising is self-serving;

it is biased and it misleads. Even comparative advertising, where one advertiser compares its wares with another, is less than desirable and hardly a serious consumer service. Without some supervision by the Federal Trade Commission and other government agencies, advertising would no doubt be worse than it is. Still, the end product of advertising agencies today can hardly be called admirable.

Many of the same points made here about newspapers and television could be made for the other media, but I will not develop an endless laundry list. Instead I will return to the criteria suggested earlier as points of comparison between and among the media. If we ask the question seriously, we find some intriguing, if depressing, answers. I recognize, of course, that any criticism of media content subjects the critic to changes of elitism. Fair enough. Measures of quality are necessarily subjective although I have tried to offer some support that goes beyond personal conjecture. My views may differ markedly from those of others. However, I would note that the American people on the one hand vote with their pocketbooks and in so doing continue to support the present output of the media. Yet, when they are allowed to make qualitative judgments they are singularly unimpressed by media content. In 1981, the Public Agenda Foundation, working with the pollster Daniel Yankelovich, conducted one of the most exhaustive surveys ever of public attitudes toward the media. The principal finding of that survey was a general public dissatisfaction with the media. The vast majority of Americans criticized the media for lack of fairness and the then-growing trend of sex and violence on television. Other studies of public confidence in the media as an institution also gave low marks to American journalism. It is true that these studies are somewhat limited and that the respondents often have little basis for comparison except their own personal standards. Still, the public is smart enough to know what it does not like.

In the realm of social consequences, I believe that the media have a more important and sustained role. Media content does get noticed and does have an impact. This may be explained by the lowest common denominator theory since the public has little real choice. The media, both print and broadcast, do have influence that is deemed important and potentially powerful. Is this power exercised to the greatest possible good? Does the press generally serve the public interest as opposed to its own narrow commercial interests?

The portrait of the content of the American mass media is not what it could be even if it is better than the norm of international standards. I personally believe that the American people are intelligent, have standards, want quality, and decry the kind of brain candy that demeans and denigrates the human spirit. To date, the American media have not gotten this message.

Merrill: Media content is generally of *good* quality and getting better.

Professor Dennis has admitted that evaluating media content is a difficult task. Certainly I would agree, but would add that pointing out negative aspects of the media and concluding general quality is poor are much easier than accentuating the positive. Media critics normally stress the weaknesses and, by and large, ignore the strengths.

The very nature of the *mass* media in America opens the door to a criticism that deprecates the general media picture, points up the rather low "common denominator" quality level of the media, which must appeal largely to the masses, and approaches media criticism from an arrogant and elitist perspective. *Generally,* of course, U.S. mass media are not paragons of quality; they do not exemplify consistently the highest standards; they do, indeed, reflect the basic characteristics of the very mass audiences they seek to serve. This is quite natural and it is also intelligent.

Again, as we have seen in other debatable issues in the arena of mass communication, we find ourselves squarely in the middle of a semantic thicket. Imprecise definitions and the whole concept of relativity circumscribe such "debates" as this one and cause the ensuing discussion to be devoid of the precision and lucidity that we might wish.

For example, we are talking about "media content." But we are not sure just which *medium* we are talking about, nor are we certain about what *content* we are specifically referring to. Beyond this, what do we mean by "generally" "poor" or "good" quality? Even though we have such questions as these about the proposition being debated and recognize that the whole issue is fuzzy around the edges, we can feel some justification for the discussion because the subject is one that constantly thrusts itself into the public forum. The American media system is an important social force and it is useful to ask questions about its quality and about the direction it seems to be going.

As I have reviewed a great wealth of critical literature about the press in recent years, I have been impressed with how poorly the press comes off. Not uncommon at all are statements similar to this harsh one by Cecil King, publisher of London's *Daily Mirror:*

I have to say that in spite of all your modernization, the American

95

> newspaper is the shabbiest product in a land which has shown
> the world how the best designed and most elegantly finished
> goods can be produced for the masses (King, 1967, p. 19).

King's indictment of U.S. newspapers, which went far beyond the above generalization about shabbiness into considerable specificity, appeared in the American *Editor & Publisher* (April 29, 1967). It was a rather good summary of the common criticisms of the American press. Even though Cecil King's criticism is from an earlier decade, his words reverberate into the 1980s. Indictments are heard on every side: about TV programs with no substance, about design and printing quality of newspapers and magazines, about sloppy writing and deficient grammar and spelling—about almost every aspect of the modern American mass media.

Professor Dennis says that when we measure American media content against what it *might be* we are likely to be disappointed. Undoubtedly. If we measure *anything* against what it might be, we are likely to be disappointed. I think we should be more realistic in our expectations; we should measure American media content against media content in the *mass media* of other countries and against the media content of past times in American history. If we do, I think we shall see that our media are very good indeed—that they are relatively vigorous, thorough, competent, literate, appealing, and useful. Any American who travels much throughout the world and has a chance to read magazines and newspapers, listen to radio, and view television will recognize that, in spite of weaknesses of American media, his media system is quite good. Professor Dennis feels the American media can only be termed "a major embarrassment." I have found that, generally, they can be termed a source of pride.

Now, I am not thinking about what they *could* be. I am thinking about them in an historical and worldwide context. Professor Dennis extols the great Muckrakers at the turn of the century and finds that modern reporters such as Woodward and Bernstein come off poorly by comparison. Dennis sees as superior to today's journalism the "good ol' days" of American journalism when "world-class performers" such as Ida Tarbell and Ray Stannard Baker produced prose and devoted great amounts of time to their projects.

Professor Dennis thinks that American journalism has progressed very little, if at all, since the turn of the century. I accept this as an opinion, but I have really seen no evidence of the superiority of earlier journalism. Dennis mentions the "strong prose" of earlier journalists like Lincoln Steffens, but just which modern journalists are being compared to Steffens? Scotty Reston, George Will, William Buckley, Norman Podoretz, Nicholas von Hoffman, Tom Wicker? We are not told. We can, of course, pick certain journalists from *any* age and use them to make a case that the journalism of that age was superior to another. But this is not very convincing.

There was, perhaps, a certain sophistication and low-keyed charm to the journalistic prose of yesteryear. But does this make that journalism more qualitative then today's journalism? You might find examples of good and forceful writing at the turn of the century or during the exciting Civil War period, but you will also find notable examples of sloppy interviewing, gap-filled stories, liberties taken with the facts, instances of fictionalizing, personal reportorial involvement and obvious bias, questionable ethics, and on and on. Certainly the American people were not informed as thoroughly and continuously at earlier periods as they are today. Journalistic quality cannot simply be limited to writing style or "forceful prose" attributed to a small sample of journalists. But this is what Professor Dennis has tried to do.

From my study of elite newspapers and those aspiring to be high quality news-oriented newspapers, both in the United States and abroad, I am convinced that the United States has a sizable group of serious, well-edited newspapers with staffs of considerable sophistication motivated to great public service. I believe that the number of such reputable, qualitative newspapers is larger than ever before. And I know of no other country in the world with such a high proportion of qualitative middle-level or "mass" newspapers. The reader of a daily newspaper in a city of 50,000 in the U.S. gets at least four times as much news as a counterpart would get if he were reading a paper in a similar city abroad. The United States has nothing to be ashamed of *generally* (and note that "generally" is part of the proposition for debate) when compared with media in other countries or media at other periods.

I invite the reader to take a trip abroad and look at the media situation. Do not just go to Paris or London, Tokyo, Frankfurt, or Zurich. Go to some small cities or towns of 10,000 to 20,000. Watch TV. Read the local newspapers. Take a look at the magazines and journals which are available. Note the superficiality of news treatment. Notice how few pages the publications have. Compare in your mind what you are getting in the way of information there and what you would be getting in the United States—wherever in the U.S. you might be.

Go to a city even in an advanced European country such as Switzerland or West Germany; visit a city comparable to Louisville, St. Petersburg, Dallas, or San Jose. See what kind of journalism you are exposed to. You will come away with a more positive feeling toward the media system of the United States. We need to remember, I think, that familiarity often breeds contempt and that quaint foreign practices do, indeed, often have undue appeal. This is why foreign media do often seem more to our liking (at least in the short run) than do our own media. But for an American foreign traveler, it does not take long after returning from abroad for the realization of U.S. media superiority to manifest itself.

Professor Dennis in his "challenge" sets up four criteria or determinants for "quality performance" by the media. Let us briefly look at these four which he has evidently used to conclude that the U.S. media system is an embarrassment:

1. *Beauty* (as expressed in design, presentation, and format. Is Professor Dennis's determination that the American media system is of poor quality and getting worse based, in any sense, on the concept of *beauty*? If so, he presents no evidence of faulty design, presentation, and format.

2. *Literary style* (as expressed in writing for print or for the electronic media). Is Professor Dennis's determination of low quality really based on evidence of poor "literary" writing? If so, he presents no evidence of poor writing *generally* (or even in specific cases). He gives some opinions on certain aspects of this (dealing with muckraking), but really makes no comparisons.

3. *Universal appeal* (of those elements that touch the heart or mind and have a lasting impact). Is the American media system of poor quality, in Professor Dennis's opinion, because it has no elements which "touch the heart or mind and have a lasting impact"? Certainly some "hearts" or "minds" are touched by messages emanating from our media system. Sociologists and psychologists—not to mention pragmatic advertising specialists would maintain that the American media have as many *universal appeals* as ever and certainly as many as can be found in the

media systems of any other country. No evidence can be found to show that these appeals, even if they are not increasing, are diminishing. For our media system to be getting worse— qualitatively worse—as Professor Dennis contends it is, it would have to show that, among other factors, the universal appeals are diminishing.

4. *Impact* (as seen in the long-term contribution of the material that is produced). Impact of the media, like universal appeals, has evidently been inferred by Professor Dennis and others who hold that this is a determinant of media quality. Certainly no evidence of lack of impact, or even of lessening impact, has been given in Professor Dennis's "challenge." I think that almost anyone familiar with the scope and potency of American mass media would be inclined to assume *great* impact (and even growing impact) of these media. Just what Professor Dennis means by "the long-term contribution of the material that is produced" is unclear, but I would suggest that *long-term* implies that the contemporary American mass media cannot be faulted in this respect *yet*. Critics like Professor Dennis will have to wait for the "long-term" to see what contribution today's media material will make to society.

Professor Dennis puts good writing very high in his criteria of quality. And he finds the American press deficient in good writing. "Good writing," he says, "is the exception, not the rule." I would agree with this, but I would add that it is the exception *everywhere,* not just in American journalism. And only an unrealistic person would expect the best writing to be found in the *mass* media; less than the very best writing is almost implied in the mass media concept. It appears to me unfair and unreasonable to even expect consistently good writing in the American press. As is true everywhere, some writing is good, some is not so good, and some is poor. Writing for the mass media is obviously not as consistently good as it could be. But I can just as well say that it is not as consistently bad as it could be, either.

Tom Winship of the *Boston Globe* is quoted by Professor Dennis to give evidence that writing in the American press is poor. Good writing, says Winship, "is always experimental." Just what does that mean? Would not such a statement simply be based on (have meaning because of) what one means by "experimental"? How is such a statement helpful in identifying good writing? Winship says that journalists need to try new forms, new subjects, new voices, stories written and reported at new distances, stories that are shorter than usual and longer than usual. When does a "new" form become old? How often do new forms need to come along before the old ones cease being good writing? How do new subjects and new voices determine good writing? How does the distance at which stories are written contribute to quality? Professor Dennis does not let Mr. Winship answer such questions, nor does he attempt answers himself.

If media critics are expecting Faulkners and Hemingways to be writing the run-of-the-mill journalistic pieces for print and broadcasting today, they are, of course, living in a fool's paradise. If this is what they expect, it is easy to see why they think the American media content is generally poor.

What we need in this country are media critics who are realistic in their criticism. It does no good to insist that an impossible "literary" face be given to the American press and that outstanding literary stylists produce the general contents of the country's media. This has never been the case and it will never be the case. The modern mass media comprise a greedy giant that consumes writing at such a pace that it is logically impossible for the highest literary quality be generally maintained. This would seem to me to be self-evident.

Bagdikian, Ben. "The American Newspaper Is Neither Record, Telegram, Examiner, Observer, Monitor, Mirror, Journal, Ledger, Bulletin, Register, Chronicle, Gazette, Transcript, nor Herald of the Day's Events ... It's Just Bad News," *Esquire,* (March 1967).

Barbato, Joseph A. "What Is a Good Newspaper?" *The Quill* (October 1965), 24–25.

Burgoon, Judee and Michael, and Charles Atkin. *What is News? Who Decides and How?* A Report of the Newspaper, Readership Project, Michigan State University (1982).

Curran, James, Michael Gurevitch, and James Woolcott, eds. *Mass Communication and Society* (Beverly Hills, Cal.: Sage, 1978.

Fiske, John. *Introduction to Communication Studies* (New York: Methuen, 1982).

Gans, Herbert. *Popular Culture and High Culture: An Analysis of Taste and an Evaluation of Taste* (New York: Basic Books, 1974).

Hulteng, J. L. *The News Media: What Makes Them Tick?* (Englewood Cliffs, N.J.: Prentice-Hall, 1979).

Kempton, Murray. "The Sound of Tinkling Brass: A Skeptical Opinion of the Press," *Harpers* (August 1974), 41–44.

King, Cecil H. "An English View of American Newspapers," *Editor & Publisher* (April 29, 1967). pp. 19, 98–99.

Luedtke, Kurt. "An Ex-newsman Hands Down His Indictment of the Press," *The Bulletin of the ASNE* (May–June 1982), 16–18.

Lyons, Louis M. "A Commentary on the Press," *Nieman Reports* (June 1972).

Markel, Lester. "Why the Public Doesn't Trust the Press," *World* (August 15, 1972).

Merrill, J. C. " 'Quality' Daily Journalism: An Analytical Discussion," *Gazette* (Holland), XV, 1, 1969.

_____. *The Elite Press* (New York: Pitman, 1968).

_____, and Harold Fisher. *The World's Great Dailies* (New York: Hastings House, 1980).

Williams, Raymond. *Communications* (Harmondsworth, England: Penguin, 1976).

Winship, Thomas. "The Care and Feeding of Writers." *Nieman Reports* 2 (Summer 1982), *36*, 19–22.

Journalistic Objectivity

8

If there is a single most important tenet of journalistic practice in the United States, it is the concept of objectivity. To some, objectivity does not mean clinical or scientific precision, but instead an effort by journalists to produce news stories and newscasts that are emotionally detached and that separate fact from opinion. Objectivity in journalistic practice is often associated with the inverted pyramid news story (news organized in a descending order of importance) and with the 5Ws and H (who, what, where, why, when, and how) or other systems of sorting out the facts necessary to convey the essence of an event or issue in an orderly fashion.

Objectivity to many means factual reporting, straightforward descriptive presentation. In recent years, though, objectivity as a theory of journalism has also included analytical reporting that goes well beyond simple description. Objectivity is a distinguishing feature of American journalism, especially when compared with journalistic content in other countries and cultures. At least that is what objectivity's proponents believe, and it has become the standard wisdom. While some of the world's newspapers engage in the presentation of polemic and opinionated essays, the U.S. approach generally has been to keep the views of the journalist segregated from the story of an event and to keep factual news on the news pages and opinion on the editorial pages.

Most critics of journalistic objectivity, as well as its defenders, agree that objectivity is a high-minded value. Some see it as a helpful goal; others see it as an unrealistic and even harmful one. Many of the so-called "new" journalists and "existential" journalists scoff at this journalistic pretense of objectivity. Still, even they would argue that American journalism generally is journalism without ideology, where method goes far toward dictating factual presentation. But there is much controversy here, and the debate goes on.

Merrill: Journalistic objectivity is *not* possible.

Many readers may think that my position—that journalistic objectivity is not possible—is like building a straw man and then proceeding to demolish it. They will say that nobody contends that journalistic objectivity is possible, and that such a "debate" as this simply turns into an exercise of semantic frustration.

First, let me say that I sympathize with such a position just attributed to "many readers," but I believe that we cannot ignore such an important journalistic concept. If we did, we would be doing an injustice to a legitimate concern of those who are involved with modern journalism—all of us. Secondly, many journalists and others talk and write as if they believe in journalistic objectivity. If they do not believe in it, then I propose that they stop using the term.

Perhaps the concept of journalistic objectivity is a "straw man" to those who seriously think about it, who are sophisticated, and who are realistic about the realties of journalism. But I contend that such persons are not legion, and that, generally, laymen and journalists alike actually think that a news story can be "objective" or that there are objective reporters out there somewhere who can be identified as different from other reporters. Certainly we hear the term used often: "I wish he had written an objective story of that speech" or "Scotty Reston—now *there* is an objective reporter."

Let us consider "objective reporting" for a minute. It would be reporting that is detached, unprejudiced, unopinionated, uninvolved, unbiased, and omniscient—and infallible, I presume. Where do we find this? The objective report would, in effect, match reality; it would tell the truth, the whole truth, and nothing but the truth. Where do we find this kind of reporting? No reporter knows the truth; no reporter can write a story which can match reality, for as the general semanticists point out, the "map is not the territory." The story, in other words, is never what it purports to be; it is always much bigger than its verbal image.

All reporters, in addition to being limited in their objectivity by the weakness of language, are also *conditioned* by experience, by intelligence, by circumstance, by environment, by physical state, by educa-

104

tion, and many other factors. They do not come to their stories as blank sheets of paper on which the reality of events is to be written. They may want to be unprejudiced, balanced, thorough, and completely honest in their reporting, but they simply cannot be.

Many believe that reporters are objective when they are *detached* from the event being covered. The problem here, of course, is what is meant by detachment. Detached in the sense of being "outside" the event being reported? Detached in the sense of being uncommitted to any of the positions involved in the event being reported? Detached in the sense of being uninterested (or disinterested) in the event except as something to be reported? Detached in the sense of holding one's self aloof from the event? Detached in the sense of making sure the reporter's point of view does not impregnate the story?

The obvious answer to all of the above questions is that it is really impossible to be detached, that the reporter's subjectivity—values, biases, interpretations, and news judgments—always enter into the production of the story.

Let me mention briefly short remarks by three journalists on this subject; they abjure any pretense of a nonsubjective viewpoint:

> *David Brinkley:* "If I were objective, or if you were objective, or if anyone was, we would have to be put away somewhere in an institution because we'd be some sort of vegetable. Objectivity is impossible to a human being."
>
> *Frank Reynolds:* "I think your program has to reflect what your basic feelings are. I'll plead guilty to that."
>
> *H. L. Mencken:* "We talk of objective reporting. There is no such thing. I have been a reporter for many years, and I can tell you that no reporter worth a hoot ever wrote a purely objective story. You get a point of view in it.

These brief opinions are representative of some journalists, but I doubt that very many journalists really would say such things—at least for public consumption. If journalists do not really believe in objective reporting, they should stop talking and writing as if they do. They should talk more about being accurate, about being as thorough as possible, about trying to keep overt or obvious opinions or judgments *of theirs* out of their stories. In other words, they should evidence the fact that they are really *aware* of the fact that "objectivity" in journalism does not exist.

Of course, there may really be some who actually think that objectivity is possible in journalism. How they come to such a belief baffles me, but I often get the impression that there are such believers. Somehow they seem to think that if a reporter checks the facts, verifies all statements, eliminates all first-person pronouns, makes an attempt to present "both sides" (as if there were only two sides) of the story—then the story is objective.

The actual state of affairs is this: Every journalist—reporter as well as editorial writer—subjectivizes his journalism. He cannot be objective, even if he would like to be. Every article, every sentence, every newscast, every movement before the camera, every voice inflection on radio is *subjective*. Even the so-called straight news reporter is subjective and his story is always judgmental, value-loaded, incomplete, and distorted as to reality. That is the nature of journalism. In fact, that is the nature of *any kind* of communication.

News reporters, even those wanting to be as aloof and neutral as possible, are caught in the natural trap of subjectivity. They involve themselves, their ideas, their values in the story—even though they may ostensibly (verbally) keep themselves out. They are in there nevertheless. They decide what aspects of the story to put in and which to leave out. They decide on the emphasis to be given various parts, which quotes to use, which parts of quotes to use, or whether to use quotes at all. When they paraphrase instead of using direct quotes they, in essence, become *translators* and their interpretive powers come into play. Although this is not objective reporting, there is really nothing intrinsically wrong with it.

Michael Novak, writing about the journalist and objectivity, makes the following pertinent observations:

> The myth of objectivity leads to ... misunderstandings in American journalism. There are no facts "out there" apart from human observers. And human observers become not more, but less astute when they try to be neutral. ...
>
> Reporters and newscasters know that if they aim at objectivity, at presenting "the facts" without editorializing, they run the risk of giving dignity to nonsense, drivel, and outright lies. What really happened in an even is not, they know, discovered by some neutral observation machine, not even by a camera. Events are not events until they are interpreted by human beings. ... To list statistics, or outwardly observable happenings, or quotations from witnesses, is to give a very narrow view of the human world.

It is to offer interpretation and editorial comment of a very
misleading sort. Reality does not come divided into "facts" and
"interpretation" (Novak, 1971, p. 40).

Novak's remarks above are in the tradition of many thinkers and
critics (e.g. Tillich, Buber, Sartre, Jaspers, Heidegger) who are in the
existentialist camp and therefore have great respect for subjectivity.
They have attacked the "emptiness" of empirical and pragmatic
objectivity beloved by Americans especially. They have said that not
only is this belief in objectivity contrary to linguistic philosophy (and
they could have said also to the principles of general semantics) but
that it demeans and devalues the individual person and the whole
concept of intersubjectivity.

I am maintaining that the whole business of journalism is really
subjective from beginning to end. And reporting is no exception. There
may be an "image" of objectivity in some stories where this image is
not obvious in others; in other words, there may be a kind of linguistic
aura of objectivity which journalists can present. But one thing is
certain: behind this aura is the reporter's subjectivity; there is *never*
any real objectivity in reporting.

Reporters are not mindless, soulless automotons, who roam about
without values, opinions, and preferences—simply soaking up reality
and spouting it out completely. They have their prejudices, their
biases, their values, their favorite topics, their heroes, and their
villains. We may wish oftentimes that there were some robotized,
completely unbiased, and blank reporters who could report "objectively," but they do not exist.

As Donald McDonald said in a seminal article ("Is Objectivity
Possible?" *The Center Magazine*, Santa Barbara, Cal., 1971), a report-
er's values are necessarily injected into the story. Of the reporter,
McDonald wrote

the value judgments he must make at every critical stage in his
investigation and interpretation of the facts must reflect the
values he already holds. Again, these values flow from his
personal history. They are products of his education, his religious
experience, his childhood, family life, social and economic background, friendships and associations, national ties and culture, as
well as his emotional life and experiences, and his reason
(McDonald, reprinted 1975, pp. 29–42).

Even beyond the influence of values on adding subjectivity news reports, one should recognize that the reporter's failure to explicate the total context keeps a story from being objective. This context in which a story happens is either not reported or it is inadequately reported. Certainly the surrounding factors of a story are part of the objectivity of the story—in short, *all* of the context is part of the story. Not only the words that a speaker speaks, but *how* the speaker says these words make up the story of the speech. Not only what he says, but what he thinks as he is speaking is part of the story—a part admittedly unavailable to the reporter at the time of the speech. But what the speaker thinks about the audience and how he feels about the audience's reaction to his speech *is* part of the speech story. (And *this* could be obtained *after* the speech by the reporter.)

Audience reaction, speaker movements, gestures, smiles, and the like form part of the objective story. The *totality* of the story is the story—the truth, the whole truth, and nothing but the truth. But the reporter realizes that he cannot give all this truth, so he strains the objectivity of portions of the story through his mental, emotional, and psychological strainer and thereby presents the audience members with a subjective account of "what happened."

Journalists are selective. They are forced by the nature of their craft to select certain facts to report, certain quotations to bring to light, certain individuals to interview, certain perspectives to give, certain aspects of an event to expose. And what happens to the other facts, individuals, perspectives, aspects in a story? Are not they also part of the objectivity of the story? The answer to the question is that many parts of the story are ignored completely. If they are not totally ignored, they are slighted, de-emphasized, or distorted in some way that keeps them from completing the objectivity of the story.

There may be something which can be called *verifiable journalism.* In other words, if as a reporter I write, "John Doe stole six cows from W. H. Arden of Winchester" and if this is indeed what happened, then that sentence is factual and verifiable. That one aspect of the story is true—in the sense that it has no overt errors in it. But when that sentence is put into a context with other sentences to make "a story," then its nonobjective nature is exposed. This sentence may be factual and as "objective" as single sentence can be, but when it is made part of a total story, then we must begin looking at the *story* and not just at the sentence.

What are the gaps in the story? What is the totality of the "story" out there in reality and what has it become in its verbal nature in the story? In essence, what happened in reality that is left out in the story? Is there a correlation between the real even and the verbal picture of the event?

It has often been said that a newsmagazine, like *U.S. News & World Report* is objective and a magazine like *Time* is not. Reason: *U.S. News & World Report* is "neutral"; it lets people speak for themselves; it often runs Q&A interviews, without going through a *USNWR* editorial "strainer" that might subjectivize them. *Time,* on the other hand, presumes to select quotes—often out of context—and to "tell" the reader what various speakers said or meant. As was said earlier, *USNWR* has been successful in presenting an "image" of objectivity, but it is doubtful that it is any more objective than any other magazine.

It subjectivizes its reportage largely through selection. One might ask: How does it select those whom it interviews in the first place? Does it not subjectivize its interviews through the questions asked by its reporter? What questions are not asked? So it may be said that the magazine has a "format" of objectivity, but beneath that format is the same old implicit subjectivity present in any journalism.

Many persons will say that journalistic objectivity is not meant to be total, that partial objectivity is what is really meant by those defending objectivity. When we consider such a "partial" concept, however, we run into trouble immediately: just how partial can objectivity be? At what point will it cease being objective?

A British provincial editor, Arnold Hadwin of Bradford, has said that total objectivity might well be impossible, but that "most people recognize and welcome objectivity that is less than total" (Hadwin, 1980, p. 29). People may welcome *something* that is "less than total" but it is not objectivity. Objectivity *is* total. And one wonders how Mr. Hadwin knows that *most people* recognize and welcome such partial objectivity. Why would people—especially most people—recognize objectivity that is less than total? Is it recognizable in *any degree* less than total? Let's say that I read a news story and say to myself: "I recognize less than total objectivity here." What have I said about objectivity or about the nature of the story? Nothing—or perhaps that I know that journalism is really always less than objective. And if it is *less than objective,* then it is *not objective.*

Armand Mattelart, a French sociologist writing from a Marxist perspective, calls objectivity the "golden rule of journalistic practice, the cornerstone of its professional deontology, and the equivalent of the Hippocratic oath" (Mattelart, 1980, p. 39). But he does not believe it. He questions the concept by saying that (1) the concept presupposes on the part of the journalist certain perceptive powers capable of penetrating reality and determining what is important and what is not; (2) the concept postulates that the description of facts (which are *what they are in themselves,* and not what the journalist *sees* them to be) goes no further than the facts themselves, and (3) facts are isolated by objectivity-oriented journalism, "cut off from their roots, deprived of the conditions which would explain their occurrence and detached from the social system which endows them with meaning and in which they possess an intelligible place" (Mattelart, 1980, p. 39).

Many writers excoriate those who, like Mattleart above, maintain that journalistic objectivity is a myth. For example, John DeMott, a journalism professor at Memphis State University, speaking at the Defense Information School at Fort Benjamin Harrison in 1976, called such people naive, foolish, and lacking in imagination. He even hinted that such persons might be subscribers to Communist theory. Some, maybe, but others, I'm sure, aren't—for example, H. L. Mencken, quoted earlier.

Professor DeMott, like many of those who claim to believe in journalistic objectivity, seems however to subscribe to a belief in the relativity or the incompleteness of "objectivity." He seems to be an absolutist—except when it comes to objectivity; then, he begins using all sorts of modifiers (like *greater* objectivity and *superior* objectivity) to weaken or lessen journalistic objectivity.

Tell the whole truth and nothing but the truth, Professor DeMott concluded in his speech: "That's objective reporting—journalistic objectivity, pure and simple." Pure and simple? Good! When I find a journalist who gives the *whole truth* and *nothing but the truth,* I will capitulate and admit that, after all, there really is journalistic objectivity.

Dennis: Journalistic objectivity *is* possible.

There is considerable irony in this debate because the prevailing view of objectivity today—shared by journalists and critics alike and persuasively summarized by John Merrill—was heresy in the 1960s. At that time (and for a thirty- or forty-year period) objectivity was the dominant philosophy that guided most of the nation's newsrooms. Those who criticized objective journalism as a myth that was beyond human capability were hooted down by defensive editors who declared that impartial and balanced reporting could be achieved and that true objectivity was a noble goal.

With great pride, Alan Barth of the *Washington Post* wrote in 1950 that "the tradition of objectivity is one of the principal glories of American journalism." Nineteen years later, Herbert Brucker of the *Hartford Courant* agreed, writing, "We can do a good job . . . as long as we keep the flag of objectivity flying high. That will give a more honest and more accurate view of this imperfect world than trusting a latter day Trotsky, or any other partisan on any side, to tell us what's what." The preceding essay reviewed some of the reasons that objectivity became an object of scorn and derision. Critics declared that "everyone is subjective and journalists have no magical powers to be otherwise." And almost everyone who had ever had a psychology course agreed.

Sometimes we forget that objectivity is merely a method and style of presenting information. Its defenders, who led the press out of a sorry period of partisan sensationalism in the 1920s, said it had three principal characteristics, namely:

1. Separating fact from opinion.
2. Presenting an emotionally detached view of the news.
3. Striving for fairness and balance, giving both sides an opportunity to reply in a way that provides full information to the audience.

What is wrong with this straightforward set of goals is that they are too simplistic and assume that complex situations can always be reduced to a balanced presentation with two alternative views. Such an approach leaves little room for ambiguity.

Beyond the underlying philosophical problems associated with objectivity was the operational difficulty in the "inverted pyramid" story which was the mode by which objective accounts were presented to the public. In its pristine form, objective news reports contain the 5Ws and H and they organize information in a descending order of importance. This journalistic style was often criticized as cold and lifeless. It was also said to obscure the truth. It was what the sociologist Gaye Tuchman called a "strategic ritual" wherein journalists used four procedures to lay claim to objectivity:

1. Presentation of conflicting possibilities.
2. Presentation of supporting evidence.
3. The judicious use of quotation marks.
4. Structuring information in an appropriate sequence.

Objectivity came under attack most significantly during the 1960s and 1970s when there was a flurry of new journalistic styles and standards. Although some of them were not altogether unknown before, they constituted a kind of journalistic movement that expressed dissatisfaction with the status quo and brought change. At the center of this movement was a vigorous assault on the concept of objectivity. Some of the developments in journalism were

1. *The New Journalism*—with writers using such literary devices as extensive description, dialogue, interior monologue, and others previously discouraged by spare-prose 5W editors.
2. *Advocacy journalism*—with its unabashed support for particular issues and causes by journalists against the impartial, objective tradition.
3. *Investigative reporting*—which took an adversarial stance and sometimes proposed solutions to problems as it uncovered corruption and moved well beyond the scope of disinterested, stenographic reporting.
4. *Service journalism or the marketing approach to news*—which employed a different definition of news, emphasizing that which is commonplace and of interest to the greatest number of people rather than that which is unique and new. With this approach, both the selection of material to be covered and the unity style aims at identifying closely with the audience. Stories aim at all

homeowners, not just unusual ones. This form of journalism (which we mention in Chapter 10) relies heavily on market research.

5. *Precision journalism*—which is the use of social science methods, including survey research, as reportorial tools to determine what is happening in the community.

All of these approaches claimed to be *more objective* than traditional objectivity. New journalists said they provided greater tone, texture, and feeling than cold, lifeless objective reports. "What we have here," said the writer Tom Wolfe, "is a subjective reality. It is really more objective than traditional reporting." Advocacy journalists also claimed that they came closer to the truth than their more conventional colleagues. "We all have a point of view," they said, "so why not admit it—up front." Journalists all too often presented facts, but missed the truth, wrote Raymond Mungo. Marketing approach journalists said, "We're giving people what they want. Our news is more pertinent and relevant." And precision journalists added, "We move beyond the limits of intuition. We use computers, statistics to give the most representative picture of the community that is humanly possible within the constraints of a news organization."

In the face of such criticism, it is no wonder that support for objectivity crumbled. While much of the criticism of objectivity as it was articulated and understood in the 1950s and 1960s is warranted, I think that it went too far. As is often the case when a prevailing mode of thought is abandoned, those who push the new view feel a need to drive a stake through the heart of the old one. In this case, it does us no service. The wave of new styles and reportorial approaches has definitely enriched American journalism, but it is time once again to look carefully at objectivity before abandoning it altogether. Objectivity fell out of favor because it was seen as an impossible goal. Maybe that judgment was too hasty. Objectivity deserves another chance. What is objectivity, anyway? According to *Webster's Third New International Dictionary,* objective means:

> ... publicly or intersubjectively observable or verifiable, especially by scientific means ... independent of what is personal or private in our apprehension or feelings ... of such a nature that rational minds agree in holding it real or true or valid ... expressing or involving the use of facts without distortion by personal feelings or prejudices. ...

Is this so wild a dream? No one would argue that journalists can achieve perfection, but is it impossible within the context of human frailty to try to be disinterested, not meaning uninterested or indifferent, but impartial? Is it impossible to observe and report those perceptions so that others can verify them if they choose to do so? Can we not reach some consensus about what is happening in our neighborhoods or communities and still leave room for differing interpretations and speculative views? To all of these questions, I would answer with a resounding "yes."

I believe that journalistic objectivity is possible if we adopt methods that lead to systematic decisions. We can borrow from some of the admirable new styles that have emerged in recent years and use the tools of rational decision making. This need not be a complex scholarly endeavor that is well beyond the daily resources of the media, but a practical and practicable strategy that will make journalism better and more reliable. I would do this in three ways: first, through strategic planning in the reporting process; second, through the use of systematic tools to analyze communities and gather information; and third, through the clear delineation of the presentation form used.

Strategic Planning

For a number of years now American corporations have engaged in strategic planning. They have corporate strategies that involve an agreed-upon approach, an understanding of the major decision-making points, and a well-calibrated effort to make the best possible choices. The relation of benefit to cost is always a central concern. Practical decisions are made with the expectation they will yield the best possible results. What we can learn from this approach in journalism is that news gathering and news making involve choices that can be made on a rational basis. They need not be purely subjective. Writer Ronald Buel says that news is essentially data that must be made into a product. This process involves a series of interrelated decisions. (Buel's framework is in italics below.)

1. *Data assignment: What is worth covering and why?* This will depend on the type of publication and its purpose. If the purpose of a newspaper is to cover the whole community as adequately as possible, then it is not difficult to inventory various components of community

114

life. This categorization may mean moving away from the old beat system that emphasizes what happens in public buildings (the courthouse, etc.) and to consider such issues as life style, the work place, business, fads and trends, the environment. Within the paper's particular definition of news, it is not difficult to make rational decisions that can be defined and justified. For example, in the coverage of a political campaign, the paper should be able to explain how it covered various candidates, why some were deemed more important than others. This ought to result in a view of the race with which other observers would concur if given the paper's original assumptions about news. It would also take into account such economic factors as staff size.

2. *Data collection: When has enough information been gathered?* Again, this is a matter of definition. But there are reasonable standards by which trained reporters know when they have assembled enough information to answer the key questions that make a complete story. Again, outsiders looking in ought to be able to understand the basis for decisions. The test here is whether, within the goals of a particular story, all of the critical questions have been answered with evidence from appropriate sources. This standard of "reasonable completeness" is frequently used in defense against libel suits and news organizations are increasingly being asked to explain their "thresholds" for finished work.

3. *Data evaluation: What is important enough to be put into a story?* Once information is gathered, only part of it can typically be included in the story. What part? And why? Sometimes new reporters make a priority list, especially if they are asked to cut a long story to meet the space demands of an editor who cannot accommodate their first submission. This decision ought to be rational. If, for example, a reporter is covering a trial, it is not difficult to list basic facts, key sources, and interpretations. If this list must be reduced markedly, the real test is what is essential to full and accurate presentation.

4. *Data writing: What words and images will be used?* Good writing means imaginative writing, which involves interpretations that are not always verifiable. Writing adds tone and complexity of perception. Still, it is not difficult to write in such a way that the writer's impressions, legitimately expressed, are distinguished from purely

115

factual information. This technique will provide a somewhat subjective portrait, of course, but still it ought to come close to what an average reader might have ascertained had he been on the scene. After all, journalists writing for mass media (as opposed to literary or specialized publications) should use words and images that are generally understood rather than engaging in brooding Jamesian analysis.

5. *Data editing: Which story should get a big headline and go on the front page or begin a broadcast and which stories should be buried, which should be changed, and which should be cut?* Again, we return to the "corporate strategy" of the news organization. What is most vital to the audience? Once that is understood, decisions can be made about cutting material or providing emphasis. The underlying policies of media organizations are based on values. These may be that news of government is more important than that of business because it affects more people, or whatever. Nonetheless, it is important that orderly, consistent decisions be made so that readers have a clear understanding of the rules of the game. Naturally values always play an important role. It is not possible to have universal answers to the questions raised in the Buel framework for all societies. The appropriate response in Lagos, Nigeria, will not be the same as that in Austin, Texas.

Mode of Presentation

There are at least three general types of journalistic presentation that ought to be considered. The chart on page 117 explains.*

Descriptive stories can easily be verified. Certain facts are presented and can be corroborated—even if there is disagreement about details. With analytical stories, we can usually inventory possible sources on a given topic. They can be listed and individual views can be set forth. The reporter brings an interpretive or sense-making perspective to the story, but this can be discerned by any one who reads the story carefully. Also, if the reporter omits a possible source, the reader should be able to see this and evaluate accordingly. Consequential

*From Everette E. Dennis and Arnold H. Ismach, *Reporting Processes and Practices, Newswriting for Today's Readers* (Belmont, Cal.: Wadsworth, 1981, p. 171.)

Three Models for News Reporting and Writing Feature Stories

	Characteristics: Uses	Questions Answered	Examples
Descriptive story	A straightforward description of the basic facts of a situation or event—terse, to-the-point, spare writing; the minimum requirements to make sense to the reader. The nature and scope of the event or issue, major sources.	Who What Where When	Spot news stories, event coverage, singular instance coverage (e.g., natural disaster, election, parade, demonstration)
Analytical story	A story focusing on the forces at work, the competing interests, points of view, possible explanations and interpretations of how and why the situation or event occurred.	How Why	Backgrounders explaining the forces (seen and unseen) behind the event or issue; shows how multiple sources, different views influenced event (e.g., stories chronicling a political decision)
Consequential story	What the story means, both currently and in the long term. Sometimes speculative, based on authoritative sources. What consequence does it have for individuals? The community? Others?	So What	Interpretive stories that grapple with meaning of issues, events, problems. Useful in trend coverage, process stories; sometimes speculative future reports (e.g., what a tax reform will mean to citizens).

stories are trickier, but they too can be presented impartially as statements of conjecture and speculation.

Armand Mattelart would no doubt see this process as astoundingly presumptuous with journalists having superhuman powers to penetrate reality. But, then, the very act of being a journalist, of presuming to report what is happening, is by definition presumptuous. However, this process is the social function of journalism and it can be done systematically in a manner that withstands examination. The true test is whether reasonable people in the same cultural setting would have similar—if not always the same—perceptions of the event or issue if they were to have done their own reporting. Certainly a highly trained lawyer will see a trial differently from the average person, but this difference does not negate the fact that mass communication aims at the mass audience and tries to make connections with a norm. The press is the surrogate of the people in our society—it represents them as their eyes and ears—and it has an obligation to present intelligent and understandable reports that give a reasonably representative picture of society. Objectivity in journalism or science does not mean that all decisions do not have underlying values, only that within the "rules of the game" a systematic attempt is made to achieve an impartial report.

Boshco, Bernard. *Newsmaking* (Chicago: University of Chicago Press, 1975).

Cohen, Stanley, and Jock Young, eds. *The Manufacture of News* (Beverly Hills, Cal: Sage, 1973).

Dennis, E. E., and A. H. Ismach. *Reporting Processes and Practices: Newswriting for Today's Readers* (Belmont, Cal: Wadsworth, 1981). See especially Chapters 1–2.

DeFleur, M. L., and E. E. Dennis. *Understanding Mass Communication* (Boston: Houghton Mifflin, 1981). See especially Chapter 12, pp. 417–445.

DeMott, John. "The News Media's Quest for Objectivity," *Vital Speeches of the Day,* Vol. 42, No. 24 (October 1, 1976), 744–767.

Epstein, Edward Jay. *Between Fact and Fiction: The Problem of Journalism* (New York: Vintage Books, 1975).

Gans, Herbert. *Deciding What's News* (New York: Pantheon, 1979).

Hadwin, Arnold. "Objectivity Is Crucial—But Is It Possible to Be Objective?" *Journalism Studies Review* (Cardiff, U.K.), (July 1980).

Hunt, Todd. "Beyond the Journalistic Event: The Changing Concept of News," *Mass Comm Review* 1 (April 1974), 23–30.

Mattelart, Armand. *Mass Media, Ideologies, and the Revolutionary Movement* (Atlantic Highlands, N.J.: Humanities Press, 1980). See especially discussion of objectivity, p. 37 ff.

McDonald, Donald. "Is Objectivity Possible?" In J. C. Merrill and Ralph Barney, eds., *Ethics and the Press* (New York: Hastings House, 1975). pp. 69–82.

Merrill, J. C. "Objective Reporting: A Myth, However Valuable . . ." *The Quill* (July 1969), 26–27.

_____. *The Imperative of Freedom* (New York: Hastings House, 1974. See especially "Quest for Objectivity," pp. 156–161.

Novak, Michael. *The Experience of Nothingness* (New York: Harper Colophon Books, 1971). See especially discussion of objectivity, pp. 37–40.

Rubin, Bernard. *Media, Politics, and Democracy* (New York: Oxford University Press, 1977). See especially Chapter 1.

Tuchman, Gaye. "Objectivity as Strategic Ritual: An Examination of Newsmen's Notions of Objectivity," *American Journal of Sociology* 4 (January 1972), 77, pp. 660–667.

News-Gathering Tactics

9

Deeply rooted in American journalism is the notion of the *journalistic reporter.* Reporters are trained in the journalistic method which gives them the tools and wherewithal to cover almost any situation they may confront. Essentially journalistic training means knowing how to gather the news— how to sift through documents, do background research, interview sources, and so on—and how to write it using the usual news and feature forms employed by newspapers and broadcast outlets.

In the midst of this seemingly routinized task, however, come all kinds of ethical issues (tactical decisions) including "checkbook journalism," fabrication of sources, false identification, lying. Some of these issues, being topical, come and go. But many are recurrent.

As with news-gathering methods and writing methods, competent reporters and editors are expected to handle tactical or ethical dilemmas. But do these problems require precise and differing tactics for different situations, or responses based on *consistent and universal* standards? While such questions are regarded as worthy of debate and discussion, most reporters believe that they have somehow internalized professional values, and competencies that will help them resolve any problems that may occur.

Merrill: Tactics should be situational and relative.

We come now to discuss a very real and important everyday concern of journalists: reportorial tactics, journalistic ways and means of gathering and writing stories. Should these tactics be situational and relative *or* should they be, as Professor Dennis will argue later, consistent and universal? I maintain that they are situational and relative; even more, I insist that they *should* or *ought to be* situational and relative. This position, of course, gets us into the realm of ethics.

Opposing my view, however, is a considerable theoretical tradition in this country, even if it fails to manifest itself in common practice. It is safe to say that an accepted truth in American journalism is that journalists should be consistent in their methods and their actions: that they should all subscribe to universal standards, and should, if they are responsible and "professional," have a profound respect for predictable and consistent practice. Consistency and predictability, we are led to believe, are foundation stones of professionalism.

Unpredictability is associated, on the other hand, with amateurism, with inconsistency and relativity, which are seen by many as deleterious to journalism, harmful to the journalist, and frustrating to the audience. I would maintain just the opposite: that consistency in journalism—the journalist always using the same tactics and dealing with the elements of the story in the same way—makes for a deadly dull journalism, keeps the individual journalist from full self-realization, and prevents the audience from being exposed to the multifaceted, rich, and diversified aspects of similar (but different) stories.

Perhaps it is more comfortable and satisfying for journalists to have hard-and-fast rules as to tactics of reporting. This proposition seems reasonable, but I cannot believe that it is either in the best interest of the newsperson or the public to have the press tied to an absolute tactical system. Most printed codes of ethics fail because they present absolute and consistent rules or standards (or because they are so fuzzily written that they, in essence, say nothing meaningful). But, perhaps, the fact that they fail is paradoxically a good thing—for their failure assures that tactical situationalism and relativism will thrive in the absence of absolute ethical codes.

Ethics, of course, is very closely related to the subject of journalistic tactics. One cannot really separate them. Should I lie, either to get a story or while telling the story to my readers or listeners? Should I reveal the source of certain statements or quotes which I use in my story? Should I give my readers or listeners all of the information which I have collected and verified?

These are just a sampling of questions that are both ethical and tactical. I might rephrase them thus:

- Should I *ever* lie as a reporter?
- Should I *always* reveal my sources? (Or *never* reveal them?)
- Should I tell the *whole truth* (as much of it as I have verified) to my audience?

Here we have introduced the possibility of tactical consistency or absoluteness. Such consistency has a notable appeal. If I am going to reveal the source in one case, why should I not reveal all sources? If I am going to lie in one case, why not in all? If I am going to withhold part of a story in one case, what would be wrong with withholding parts from any story?

Let me give an example of each of the two tactical positions:

1. Absolute: *always* identify victims of *all* crimes.

2. Relativistic: identify victims in *some* crimes but not in others.

The first tactic (the absolute) does, indeed, simplify the journalist's decision making. If this tactic is accepted all that must be done is to identify all victims—juveniles, the mentally ill, rape victims, and so on. The second tactic (the situational) is more difficult because it forces the reporter to discriminate, to think. The reporter must see distinctions, think about consequences; in short, the reporter must decide that it is not only all right but good journalism to make exceptions—to have double standards, if you will.

The reporter who is situational recognizes that there is a difference, and a very important one, between a rape victim, for example, and a murder victim. Naming a rape victim can bring mental and emotional harm to the victim; naming a murder victim cannot harm the victim at all. The thinking reporter understands that the naming of a nine-year-old boy for shooting his father is quite different (in psychological, if not in legal, terms) than the naming of a 39-year-old adult for shooting his father. The reporter believes that it is his duty to make certain editorial decisions impinging on what is and is not published. After all, he reasons, editorial decision is the nature of journalism: selection is made to some degree—among facts in *every* story that is written.

I contend that a reporter must play this tactical game rather loosely; that he must not strive for consistency in tactics; that he must consider the specific situation or circumstance. In short, the reporter (to be effective and in many cases to be ethical, too) must specifically determine *not* to be absolute and consistent, but rather to be situational and relative.

Case: A reporter cannot subscribe to a tactic of always revealing his source—even if he does, indeed, maintain that the people have a right to know. In some cases, to reveal sources would be counterproductive as well as unethical. For example, the journalist may get information from a source who would be in great physical danger if his identity were known. The reporter not only wants to keep the source operative for another day, but also to avoid endangering his life. In other, similar cases, the reporter might want to keep his source from losing his job.

Case: A reporter is writing a rape story. He has the name of the person arrested on suspicion of committing the rape. He also has ascertained the name of the rape victim. He decides not to use the victim's name, although he does not hesitate to use the suspected rapist's name. Inconsistent? Yes. He is, in effect, withholding information from the reader. At the same time he is providing the name of another person connected with the case—even though this person may not have committed the rape. He feels no qualms about this procedure, even though it is inconsistent, reasoning that in this particular case it is tactically prudent to do as he has done. He justifies withholding verified information from the reader on ethical grounds—on a consideration of possible consequences to the victim.

The reporter in the above case is inconsistent. And he certainly does not subscribe to a "universal" tactic. A universal tactic in reporting would be: The reporter is obligated to report all the facts that he has, all that he has verified, and all that are pertinent to the story. Period.

In this rape story, certainly the name of the rape victim is *pertinent to the story*, as we will be told by our absolutist reporter. After all, the reporter has found out who the woman is; therefore should not the name be given—especially since the name of the rape suspect has been used?

Let me reply to the above question with another question: Why *should* the reporter use the victim's name? The reporter is wise to subscribe to relativistic tactics, to play the story the way he wants to play it in that particular case—after consideration of possible consequences. Why should the reporter *always* name names? Why should the reporter subscribe to the same tactics in every story? Straightjacketing oneself does not assure better reportage by the reporter. In fact, a relativistic or situational tactical program in reporting is what is called for. Consider each story. Consider the ramifications of each story. Consider the importance of the story. Consider consequences or implications for certain persons in the story (e.g., the rape victim in the example above).

It may well be that when a reporter considers the importance to the public of a particular story, there will be a realization that "usual" tactics must be modified or changed. The reporter may decide that the story is important enough, for example, to steal files (or at least to make copies of papers and return the files). The reporter may even feel that in a particular case there is justification to pose as someone else. It may be that the reporter will decide to eavesdrop on conversations and report what he overhears, using or perhaps not using the names of those who said the things he is divulging. The reporter might decide to "bug" a room or wiretap a telephone in order to get some very important information which he believes the public should know. The reporter might decide, in order to get some much-needed information, to tell a source that he knows certain things or that he has heard certain things from someone else (which he really has not heard) in order to get a response. The reporter might decide to make up quotes and drop them into a story so as to prompt someone connected with the story—someone he wants to make a statement—to come forward to refute or to enlarge on the "speculated" or fabricated quotes.

Now, we can justify these tactics by resorting to the "ends justifies the means" argument. We can say that we are thinking of the public, and the public's right to know. How can the public know unless we break through the barriers of secrecy with our situational tactics? So, journalists must resort to these tactics *from time to time* in order to do their job, to live up to their responsibilities.

We can justify relativistic or situation tactics by contending that they are more ethical; we can also justify them instrumentally or pragmatically by saying that they are needed to accomplish our ends. If we need a further rationale for inconsistency in journalistic practice, we can always fall back on press freedom in its editorial self-determinism sense. In other words, it is the right of a newspaper reporter to be inconsistent; if he wants to use a victim's name (or any name) in one story and not in another, that is his right.

If the reporter wants to reveal the source of a quote in one story and not in another, that is his right. In fact, if the reporter wants to reveal the source of a quotation in one part of a story and make all the other quotes in the same story anonymous, that is his right.

After all, why *should* the reporter be consistent or use universal tactics? Even though there may not be any evidential basis for the belief, the reporter can contend that journalistic consistency is the "hobgoblin of little minds." Journalism, it seems to the relativistic reporter, is riddled with instances of inconsistency, most of which are considered valid journalistic practices. Here are just a few:

- Using the 5W lead in one story, but not in another.
- Using indirect quotations *only* in one story, and using direct quotations or a mixture of indirect and direct quotes in another.
- Giving the addresses of persons in one story, and omitting addresses in another.
- Going directly to persons for information in one story, while going to someone for second-hand information in another or using old information from the files.
- Giving certain personal data (such as age, race, occupation) about some persons in some stories but not about other persons.

A list of inconsistent tactics could be extended easily. What is the alternative to these inconsistent tactics? Consistent and universal tactics, we are told. The intelligent and dedicated reporter can only scoff at such an alternative, seeing it as a definite voluntary placement of the reporter in a straightjacket with little chance to achieve a primary goal of journalism: obtaining the story.

Why, asks the dedicated reporter, should I *never* deviate from a kind of traditional tactical program? If the normal tactics will not work, why not use others that will work?

I may *usually* want to give sources for information in my story. But why must I always give them? I may *usually* want to avoid deceiving a person to get information, but why not deceive when I feel the issue is important enough to warrant deception? I may *usually* want to identify myself as a reporter, but there will be times when I need either to hide my identity or to pass myself off as someone else. I may *usually* want to get my interviews free—as part of a newsstory—but why should I not pay someone for an interview if I feel my news medium wants it or that it is important to the public?

In short, I am not wise or very sophisticated if I *always* use the same tactics. Consistent and universal tactics are simply not instrumentally (or ethically, in many cases) conducive to effective journalism nor are they in line with a journalist's dedication to getting the story and keeping the public informed.

Dennis: News-gathering tactics should be consistent and universal.

The preceding discussion of news-gathering tactics defends the status quo in American journalism. Reporters do use relative and situational methods when gathering the news. However, there are many agreed-upon general standards and practices. These practical tactics for getting information are undergirded by ethical judgments that are self-contained, based mainly on the immediate situation rather than considered against the backdrop of long experience with similar cases. There is more than a slight temptation to reinvent the wheel with each ethical dilemma that arises.

That, in my opinion, summarizes one of the most serious problems in journalistic practice today—a thoughtless, seat-of-the-pants approach to reporting that eschews planning and thinking. It is the journalism of intuition. "Do what intuition tells you; apply common sense to the situation" are accepted axioms. On the face of it this doesn't sound so bad, but consider the following:

- A reporter for NBC News is asked how he knows when he has enough information to "go" with a story. "How," he was asked, "can you be sure that your information is complete, that you are not missing major sources that would turn a story completely around, maybe with a different interpretation altogether?" The reporter replied, "You just know. There is," he added, "no answer, things just click into place and it seems right."

- An editor for a metropolitan daily newspaper is asked by a Harvard Law professor how far he would go to get a story. "Would you lie? Would you steal? Would you disguise your identity?" The editor thought for a moment, then responded, "Yes, under some conditions, I'd probably do all of those things even though I might personally find some of them reprehensible." The professor wanted to know, "How do you make your decision; on what theory do you base your actions?" And the editor answered, "I have no theory, I just do what I think is right."

We would not accept this kind of thinking from other professional persons (say, doctors, lawyers, or architects) whom we expect to have standards, codes, and a systematic basis for their decisions. We do accept it from journalists perhaps because we have no choice or because they convince us that news is unpredictable, a matter of timing that requires on-the-spot decisions governed solely by the facts of a particular situation. "You simply can't quantify these things," goes the incantation.

There is a prevailing myth in American journalism that planning news coverage runs counter to freedom of the press. Planning is thought to be dull and routine, not spontaneous and timely. It is further said that writers are creative persons who, if left to their own devices, will produce a better kind of journalism. And God forbid that journalists should have hypotheses. A hypothesis, which is an assumption that becomes an organizing principle, is thought to encourage bias and run counter to journalistic objectivity (which we treated in Chapter 8). There is also a prevailing view among many journalists that news really defies precise definition.

This kind of "every day a new beginning" theme in many newsrooms, the operational rule of the status quo, needs rethinking. While it certainly is not possible to always predict with scientific certainty what will happen on a given day, journalism is really much more routinized than most of its practitioners *know* or will *admit.* They may not know it because American journalism is insulated and parochial. Many journalists have little work experience outside of their present assignments; few belong to national organizations where they come into contact with other journalists; few subscribe to professional publications or make any effort to keep up with the literature of their own field. And most sneer at the thought of reading "media sociology," systematic research that gives us data about patterns and practices across many journalistic organizations. Individual journalists may know their own organization intimately, but they often have little knowledge about the field generally. This situation is not unusual because many professionals are so busy doing their jobs that they have little time to think about them or to make comparisons with their colleagues in other places. For a field that is supposed to demand so much creative calibration, journalism is remarkably predictable, routinized, even stodgy. Send any five reporters to cover a city council story and you can predict with almost considerably certainty what they will write. Why? Because the coverage of public affairs, in particular, has been standardized. There is much agreement about the form and format of stories, about what essential facts should be included, and about what most editors will accept. Reporters know what is expected of them and generally they do it.

Of course there are stories that are more complex than routine meetings, but even with these the traditional methods of news gathering pretty much dictate what will eventually appear. And if this were not enough, we have "rewards and punishments" built into the journalistic system to guarantee conformity. At a positive level there are prizes (such as the Pulitzers) that honor imaginative work within the framework of traditional journalism. Journalism schools help out by promoting conventional approaches to news gathering through courses and books.

There is in American journalism a serious perceptual conflict. Journalists on the one hand believe that their work is unpredictable, situational, and relative. Communications researchers say this is not true, that reporting is not nearly as uncertain as practitioners think. In a sense both are right. While there may be great similarity in work patterns and output from day to day, journalists still think that there is little formal guidance and that there is considerable latitude for individual decision making. They say that with regard to ethics, they live in a conceptual thicket which requires instant decisions of convenience if not conviction. They tend to justify what they do without worrying whether their choices about revealing sources or lying are consistent with what they did before. Scholars, on the other hand, because they are trained to look for patterns of organizational and individual activity, can see a method—whether haphazard or well-thought-out—in journalistic work, just as they do in firefighters or farmers. The way the newspaper or broadcast station is organized, the selection of personnel, their training and socialization, all have a hand in shaping the news.

Interestingly enough, it is the once-similar (and now quite different) practices of journalists and social scientists that explain some of this discrepancy. As Philip Meyer, well known for his work in precision journalism and now a professor at the University of North Carolina, has written

> Social scientists used to be more like journalists. They relied on observation and interpretation, collecting the observations from public records, from interviews, from direct participation, and then spinning out the interpretations. Like many journalists they cheerfully accepted the American folk wisdom ... that anyone

with "a little common sense and a few facts can come up at once
with the correct answer on any subject" (Meyer, 1979, p. 216).

But something changed. First with the development of inferential
statistics and later with the advent of computers, social scientists no
longer worked like journalists. Instead they used powerful quantitative tools to deal with unwieldy and massive data. Now, says Meyer,
social scientists are doing "what we journalists like to think we are
best at: finding fact, inferring causes, pointing to ways to correct social
problems, and evaluating the effects of such correction" (Meyer, 1979,
pp. 216–217). In short, he charges that journalism is being left behind
because it lacks a systematic approach to news gathering. (We have
mentioned this in the preceding chapter).

The point, of course, is that with an effective strategy for gathering
information which systematically considers possible sources and mines
them with care brings a far richer yield than old-fashioned, impressionistic reporting. It is now possible to determine how much information from what sources will be adequate—when enough information
has been assembled and when writing can begin. This statement does
not mean that journalists should be exactly like social scientists. Press
people have greater time pressures and are more concerned about
immediacy.

It is one thing to develop a strategy for news coverage that lists the
tactics to be employed, another to actually do it. No situation is ever
perfect and no prearranged rules ever work in all situations. For this
reason some journalists throw out the rules altogether and make
expedient decisions. It is threatening to ask: Is the information
complete? Have I mined all possible (and reasonable) sources? Is the
evidence strong enough to warrant the conclusion—actual or implied?
Are various interpretations and leaps in logic justified? If such
questions could have been avoided in the past, such is no longer the
case.

Systematic newsgathering tactics are not simply a theory for
journalism schools to trumpet, but something being demanded by the
rest of society. One of the most compelling calls comes in the courts.
Frequently in libel suits news organizations must offer evidence that
their story has "an absence of malice." This requirement means that
the story is not marred by "knowing falsehood" or "reckless disregard"
of the truth. How is this honesty of intent determined? By showing
that reasonable efforts, consistent with national news-gathering

131

standards, were employed. If they were not and the paper admits it, there is the possibility for a whopping libel judgment. Sloppy reporting is expensive. Of equal or greater importance is the fear that journalists will not have the credibility they need and deserve unless their methods are respected by the audience.

People who argue against ethical standards or moral imperatives in news-gathering tactics usually suggest that each case is so different that rules will straightjacket the reporter. They add that general guidelines are so vague that they are meaningless. I disagree. We need a theory of journalistic ethics, a fundamental framework for reporters to base their decisions on. This framework requires general understanding about ethical behavior, whether in reporting or everyday life. It means having a clear notion about how specific journalistic dilemmas ought to be handled. This general ethical understanding does not mean that rules cannot be modified or tempered to meet particular situations. We need a thoughtful policy that serves as a conscience for individual journalists and their organizations. Such a policy should spell out standards of conduct for information gathering. One minimal standard, I think, is that journalists should obey the law. In most instances this principle means they should not lie, steal, or cheat. They should not wiretap or break into places not otherwise open to them. In rare instances, a right-thinking reporter may want to be civilly disobedient, to deliberately break the law as a matter of principle because it will lead to a greater social good. In all instances where ethical questions arise, if there is not a clear answer; reporters should consider alternatives, not simply rush to judgment with the easiest solution. If the decision runs counter to conventional wisdom and standard ethical codes, there ought to be a clear and compelling rationale for making it.

For example, in most instances it is regarded as ethical to reveal one's sources in a news story. This strengthens the credibility of the story and ties information to attributed sources. If revealing names will put sources in great danger or make them reluctant to talk, a different decision may be appropriate. If it is determined that a source should not be named, the information should meet a test of public benefit, clearly agreed upon and understood by the reporter's supervising editors so that they can defend the action later. And the reporter, if subpoenaed by the courts, must be ready to go to jail if it comes to that.

The problem today is that many reporters do not have solid ethical training and do not have the kind of foundation necessary for ethical decision making. Again, consistency is terribly important both for accountability to one's bosses and perhaps ultimately to the courts.

Journalists have gotten in trouble for being inconsistent in recent years with regard to fair-trial–free-press codes. The press was a signatory to such codes, which list tactical guidelines for covering criminal proceedings from initial investigations of crimes to court judgments. Reporters generally agree to withhold some information (such as prior arrest records) in the interest of not prejudicing a jury and assuring the defendant of a fair trial. This is a social compact between the press and the legal system. When the press violates this agreement or decides not to abide by a particular provision of the code, there ought to be a good reason (beyond curiosity seeking or pandering) to justify its action. If not, reporters and editors may have to answer in court. This happened in 1981 in a notable case in the state of Washington where a newspaper was held accountable for violation of the fair-trail–free-press code.

As this example indicates, it is always possible to substitude a "greater social good" argument or a "humanitarian" argument to explain why an individual journalist or publication may deviate from an accepted rule. I believe such exceptions should be justified on the basis of devotion to the public interest, rather than petty or self-serving reasons.

Similarly it is quite appropriate to reconsider rules that are regarded as journalistic conventions or articles of faith. Printing the names of persons involved in litigation, for example. Withholding the rape victim's name while printing that of the person accused of rape has been mentioned. This practice would seem potentially unfair both to victim and accused. The press usually prints the name of the accused. But is it really necessary? The reasons for printing names has to do with keeping the courts open so that they do not become secret tribunals. Thus, we know who is being tried, for what, and why. But as long as the courts are open to the press and to spectators, why not defer printing this material until the trail is over? No great social good is done by heralding names of victims or accused persons in advance of trial with some obscure exceptions.

Some newspapers have abandoned the practice of printing names of persons in civil litigation cases where the truly important story is the effect of the decision on similar cases in the future. If one person is suing another to establish a legal principle and if revealing names would prove embarrassing, it may serve no purpose to do so. Some wise editors are changing their policy in this area.

Consistent and universal standards of reporting with necessary escape clauses for unusual or unique situations will do much to enhance journalistic practice in America. Such standards, if widely known (and the press can virtually guarantee this with adequate coverage), will do much to strengthen public confidence in the fairness and completeness of reporting. It will also have real advantages for individual newspapers and broadcast stations in an increasingly litigious society. Haphazard, thoughtless conduct that meets no standard, but blunders along willynilly is neither appreciated nor rewarded by the courts. One of the most effective ways to put the journalistic house in order is to establish coherent policies and consistent practices. This is the essence of professionalism performance and distinguishes competent performance from rank amateurism.

FURTHER READING

Diamond, Edwin. *The Tin Kazoo* (Cambridge, Mass.: MIT Press, 1975).

Hage, George S., Everette E. Dennis, Arnold H. Ismach, and Stephen Hartgen. *New Strategies for Public Affairs Reporting,* 2nd Ed. (Englewood Cliffs, N.J.: Prentice-Hall, 1983).

Hulteng, John L. *The Messenger's Motives: Ethical Problems of the News Media* (Englewood Cliffs, N.J.: Prentice-Hall, 1976).

MacDougall, A. Kent, ed. *The Press: A Critical Look from the Inside* (Princeton: Dow Jones Books, 1972).

Merrill, John C. *Existential Journalism* (New York: Hastings House, 1977).

Meyer, Philip. *Precision Journalism* (Bloomington: Indiana University Press, 1979).

Rubin, Bernard. *Questioning Media Ethics* (New York: Praeger, 1978).

Deciding
What Is News

10

What is sometimes called the "news-making" process is the result of a daily bargaining process between and among various personnel in newspapers and broadcast stations. Editors look at the world they cover with particular standards and measures. They attempt to direct reporters to cover the most interesting and thus newsworthy material. There are some generally accepted definitions of news and these provide the justification for what appears in the newspaper and on the newscasts. Many competing forces want space in the news columns or on newscasts. Some are self-serving external persons who want their story old sympathetically and well; others are reporters who want their work in the paper; still others are subtle influences ranging from values and habits to personal preferences. A standard view is that at the bottom line news is determined by editors and that editors' (or other gatekeepers) judgments should, in fact, decide what is news. There can be no mechanical standard, it is said, because the news of the day is dynamic and its results are uncertain. Therefore, the well-trained editor or news director makes judgments reflecting prevailing journalistic practices and the specific needs of the audience as perceived by upper management. This, it is further stated, is the essence of journalistic (and other media) leadership. Even Chief Justice Burger has remarked that the job of editors is to edit.

Dennis: *Market forces,* not editors' judgments, should decide what is news.

There is a long-standing and persistent debate among media professionals and media critics about just what news is and who should make decisions about it. Editors and reporters say with much assurance that they and they alone should make decisions about news, determining what will appear in the news columns and on newscasts and what will not. Some critics of the press, for example people in business, say that the sources of news, those quoted in stories or covered in some fashion, should have a role in defining and shaping the news. In actuality, news decisions are made by journalistic professionals with little guidance from anyone, no matter how much their detractors may complain. This situation is changing, though, as intuitive judgments are being challenged more and more by market forces which we learn about most effectively through market research. In my view, this change is a good thing and I hope that before long many of today's smug, all-knowing editors will replace their seat-of-the-pants (or skirt) decisions with more thoughtful, better-researched, systematic decision-making. To such persons, this position is heresy, of course.

For as long as anyone can remember editors (with the help of various minions) have decided what will grace the pages of newspapers or appear on newscasts and what will not. They have engaged in a hard selection process, elevating some items to importance and public exposure while relegating others to the wastebasket. Editors are hired to make these judgments and for the most part they do so with the best of intentions. But how are these judgments made and are they the right ones? Against what set of criteria are news items and stories selected? On what basis are others deemed unworthy of coverage?

Most editors would tell you that they make their choices from among those news stories that they assign or that flow in from their regular channels (such as wire services) and they do so with proper regard for their audience. They would also tell you that they rely heavily on the "budgets" of the wire services (priority lists of stories deemed important or significant) as well as taking cues from such major national media as the *New York Times, Washington Post,* and the three major television news networks. What will interest the audience is of paramount importance for, after all, if readers and viewers are not attentive, newspaper circulations may drop and broadcast ratings may falter. This situation would push revenues down and the editor might be fired or see the paper die.

It came as something of a surprise to many editors when in 1947 the Commission on Freedom of the Press, a privately funded blue-ribbon group that evaluated the news media, suggested that the media were failing to give readers a representative account of the day's news, let alone present a "representative picture" of the constituent groups of society. As with most media criticism, however just, editors rejected these ideas wholesale. Still, the issue raised by the Commission continues to raise its head at professional meetings and in scholarly critiques of the media. The definition of news is the subject of much wrangling and for good reason. I believe that a new approach to news decision making is needed more than ever.

1. News is a highly complex formulation that requires the best intelligence and a thoughtful strategy for professionals to fashion it properly.
2. Editors and reporters are elitists, unrepresentative of their readers and viewers and unable to act effectively on their behalf.
3. A marketing approach to news is the most effective and efficient way to select and present news that is of interest to and pertinent for the audience.

Ask journalism students if they know what news is and they will tell you, "Yes, of course." Ask them to define it and confusion sets in. News is difficult to define, which explains why there is a lively continuing debate among many persons trying to sort it out. All kinds of people—journalists, sociologists, political scientists, news sources, and others—have engaged in this exercise. It is more than a theoretical discussion, because knowing and understanding what news is can have real payoffs. Imagine the political candidate whose idea of news differs radically from that of the local editor. The candidate is likely to quickly be a former (and defeated) candidate if that view persists. The same is true for others who want to get something into the news.

In a rather scornful view of news, Henry David Thoreau once wrote

I am sure that I have never read any memorable news in a newspaper. If we read of one man robbed, or murdered, or killed by accident, or one house burned, or one vessel wrecked, or one steamboat blown up, or one cow run over on the Western Railroad, or one mad dog killed, or one lot of grasshoppers in the winter—we never need of another. If you are acquainted with the principle, what do you care for myriad instances and applications? To a philosopher all news, as it is called, is gossip, and they who read it or edit it are old women over their tea (Thoreau, 1854, pp. 148–49).

Thoreau clearly identifies some of the negative characteristics of news. Some commentators have tried to explain the difference between facts, truth, and news with less than full success. Walter Lippmann once wrote that "news is not a mirror of social conditions, but the report of an aspect that has obtruded itself." One famous definition of news is that attributed to John Bogart of the *New York Sun* who said in 1880, "When a dog bites a man, that is not news, but if a man bites a dog, that is news!" Newscaster David Brinkley would seem to agree: "News," he said, "is the unusual, the unexpected. Placidity is not news. If an airplane departs on time, it isn't news. If it crashes, regrettably, it is."

Some of the standard criteria that are said to make up the news are

1. Conflict (tension–surprise).
2. Progress (triumph–achievement).
3. Disaster (defeat–destruction).
4. Consequences (effect upon community).
5. Eminence (prominence).
6. Novelty (the unusual, even the extremely unusual).
7. Human interest (emotional background).
8. Timeliness (freshness and newness).
9. Proximity (local appeal).

Sociologist Bernard Boshco, who wrote a distinguished book about news, says that all news has a dual origin. It is a *social* product that represents an effort to make sense out of what is happening in society and it is an *organizational* product representing what the news organization decides to do with it.

This writer and a coauthor, after reading scores of articles and treatises on news, came up with this definition that reflects some of the factors that go into news:

News is a report that presents a contemporary view of reality with regard to a specific issue, event, or process. It usually monitors change that is important to individuals or society and puts that change in the context of what is common or characteristic. It is shaped by a consensus about what will interest the audience and by constraints from outside and inside the organization. It is the result of a daily bargaining game within the news organization that sorts out the observed human events of a particular time period to create a very perishable product. News is the imperfect result of hurried decisions made under pressure (DeFleur & Dennis, 1981, p. 422).

This is not to suggest that our definition of news changes daily. It does not. There is considerable consistency over time as to what editors deem newsworthy; the similarity (some would say sameness) of our newspapers and newscasts suggests considerable agreement about what news is under most conditions.

The success of news organizations depends not only on a proper selection of news that will interest its audience but also on effective presentation (in writing styles and graphic displays, headlines, and so on) of the news.

A key factor here is the "everyman" ideal of the journalist, which supposedly applies equally to editors and reporters. It is said that they have a built-in understanding of their readers and viewers if they are any good at all in their jobs. After all, readers and viewers are the journalists' next door neighbors, friends, companions at sports. While this vision of the journalist may be true in very small communities, for the most part it is far from the mark. Editors and reporters are part of an elite. They simply are not like most of the citizens of the community. They are better educated, more liberal politically, less religious, more likely to be single, to live in an apartment (as opposed to a single-family dwelling), and to have both social and cultural values that are quite distant from others around them. National studies have documented this condition for a number of years now. They draw a portrait of journalists as relatively isolated and out of touch with their communities. As one reporter was quoted in a 1982 study:

It is an inherent problem; inbred newspapers don't trust the people they are writing about. . . . Especially the younger reporters are getting removed from society. They come from different

backgrounds than the average public. [Theirs is] a snobbish view
of the world. (Burgoon et al., 1982, p. 5)

That study, based on a national survey conducted for the American
Society of Newspaper Editors, went on to say that journalists under-
estimate reader intelligence, have a poor understanding of what people
will actually read, and simply do not comprehend the role of television
in delivering news to people who also read newspapers. The report was
a stinging indictment of the press that was not out of line with a more
impressionistic speech by Kurt Luedtke, which we have mentioned
before in this book. Luedtke charges that his former colleagues in the
media suffer from the twin perils of "arrogance and irrelevance." One
keeps them unpleasantly off the track with readers; the other could
spell doom in an era when other information sources (data banks
provided by cable systems or the telephone company) can supply much
of the factual information (sports scores, weather reports, etc.) that
people now get from newspaper and television news. There are a
number of things that editors and reporters can do to get and stay in
touch with their communities, but nothing will change the inevitable.
Journalists will continue to be elites, continue to be unlike their
readers and viewers.

But all is not lost. Like the Lone Ranger rescuing a damsel in
distress, market research can help save the day. It already is at some of
the nation's most successful (and most consistently in touch) newspapers. A marketing approach to news makes news decision making less
of a guessing game and more of a thoughtful process that takes into
account the interests and needs of the audience. In the marketing
approach this is done systematically, not on the basis of whimsical
guessing.

The marketing approach to news is really nothing new. In fact in the
1970s when newspaper circulations were sliding downward, a national
Newspaper Readership Project collected data about reader interests,
preferences, and reading habits. As a result many American newspapers changed their formats radically, offering special sections on
lifestyles, neighborhoods, and entertainment. News was packaged
differently with livelier design and more vivid writing. For example, a
news story on a zoning ordinance would begin by suggesting the
consequences of the news story for potential homeowners, rather than
simply summarizing the action of the zoning board in a procedural

manner. It would likely be displayed with striking photos or line drawings and readable, attractive headlines.

The marketing approach to news depends on a regular and accurate flow of statistical data about the audience. The data are then used as one factor, a central one, in determining what will be offered to the audience and in what manner. News is matched to the interests and potential interests of the audience. Some critics have called this approach "soft and sexy in the afternoon," suggesting that a marketing approach must always emphasize soft news rather than important news of public affairs. The best marketing approach papers, however, have an effective blend of editorial leadership wherein professional journalists make news selections and prepare material with strategies for reaching the reader. Those strategies are dependent largely on marketing research data. This process is not a mindless one where journalists succumb to hard-hearted statistics while ignoring professional ethics and a desire to be complete in their coverage of a community issue or problem. Information is a calibrating tool that, when used by intelligent people, can result in a higher quality product. Market information gives news organizations a continuous source of feedback from their readers and viewers, something that is lacking in many places today.

Naturally any discussion of the marketing approach to news revives the old debate of whether the press should give readers what they want or provide leadership that gives citizens what they need. I believe that the two are not incompatible, that the public is ultimately better served if market information plays a more important role in guiding editors' decisions. If today's newspapers need television stations guided mainly by intuition are so far out of touch, it is worth making our best effort to bridge the gap. Market information intelligently used will do it.

Merrill: *Editors' judgments,* not market forces, should decide what is news.

Unfortunately perhaps, Professor Dennis has challenged a proposition that is not contradictory to what he is advocating. What Professor Dennis seems to be saying, though he only gets to it in the last several paragraphs of his essay, is that news should be determined by a regular and accurate study of audience desires. In this sense, the audience and not the editor determines what is news. The editor, in the Dennis perspective of news, is consigned to a mechanistic role whereby he or she serves as a short-order cook preparing only what the customer orders. This is harsh pragmatism, crass capitalism carried far too far, in my opinion.

The marketing approach to news regulates the press to a powerless dispenser of desired services. Editors take on a strange role; they do not make decisions, but only grant requests. They do not determine what their audiences need or should have; rather they provide the news that the audiences—the real editors in the marketing approach—say they want. In effect, if Professor Dennis's concept of editorial leadership were taken very far, journalism would become a passive and uninspiring vocation.

Now, Professor Dennis realizes this danger, and he tries to moderate his advocacy of the marketing approach to news by conceding that the "best marketing approach papers have an effective blend of editorial leaderhip wherein professional journalists make news selections and prepare material with strategies for reaching the reader." In other words, Dennis would have editorial leadership at the same time editors follow the dictates of audience research. He wants it both ways.

If this is the case, then I have very little to argue against. For I agree that market forces enter into the editor's decisions about news. Any American journalist who has ever dealt with determining what news is and how to play it has recognized the natural symbiosis between editorial decision making and audience desires. Only the most naive person would think that the editor's judgment and the audience preferences are mutually exclusive.

What I am arguing is that the editor (or some journalistic decision maker) should decide what is news. He or she may do this whether taking audience desires into consideration or simply ignoring what he believes to be the will of the audience. In other words, market forces

144

may or may not enter into the determination of news. I see news as an editorial matter, not as a public matter. This is the main business of the editor: determining what news is and how it shall be played. Of course, he will naturally be influenced by his knowledge of the public; he knows that he is not producing his newspaper in a vacuum and that he cannot ignore the audience.

No editor has ever ignored the audience. So, in that sense at least, editorial determination of news has always taken market forces into consideration. But editors have generally prided themselves on their own ability to recognize and determine news. They have seen themselves as independent decision makers in journalism and not simply reactors and servants to their audiences. I feel that they have been justified in this image of themselves. Anybody who has worked for a news medium knows full well that the great majority of news decisions are made by journalists without evidence of what the audience wants. News is determined quickly, stories are selected from the many available without too much deliberation, and the journalists make these determinations almost instinctively. Certainly, they do not have the luxury of holding various stories in abeyance until they can survey their readers to find out which of the stories might be desired. The pragmatics of journalism militates against the marketing approach to news.

This approach does not mean that the reasonable news executive does not have some general guidelines for news based on inferences drawn over time from the audience. Professor Dennis has already presented some of the standard criteria that help determine news— and, of course, these criteria did not suddenly leap full-grown from the editor's head. Over the years, journalists came to the conclusion that *generally* these were criteria that were agreeable to news consumers. So the editors did have some overall, long-range guidelines for news; but on a daily, decision-by-decision basis, they made their own determinations as to what would be news in their news media.

As Professor Dennis says in his "challenge," all of this brings up the old debate of whether the press should give readers what they want or what they need. I believe that the press should give readers what the editors think they want *and* what they need. This is, really, what the press does. What the people want can also be what they need. What they need may not, however, be what they want—that is, unless they are made somehow to realize that there are some things they need which they have not thought about needing.

A good editor is one who recognizes that it is a journalistic responsibility to provide the reader with some significant and useful news which may or not be of great immediate interest or appeal; at the same time, the editor knows that, in order to get the reader exposed to such news, he must also provide types of news of a more shallow— perhaps even sensational—nature. The good editor is a pragmatist and a realist, not some one-dimensional person seeking either to entertain or to educate. The good editor wants to do both, and other things as well. But, in additon to being a realist, he is something of an idealist also, believing that readers should get certain information which they might not choose if given the chance. In this sense, the editor is much like an educator.

The editor may very well use marketing information for some of his decisions. Certainly he has access today to a considerable amount of such information. He may, however, decide not to use marketing data for his news determinations; in fact, he generally does not. He uses intuition, instinct, and perceptions of news value stemming from experience and common sense. Often, also, he projects his own likes and dislikes about news to his readers. This may not be scientific, but it is useful and quick—and it works very well. The editor is a kind of one-person sample, projecting to his newspaper the news values of himself as a representative of his community. As such, the editor can retain at least the illusion of independent editorial news determination while taking into consideration the assumed interests and desires of the audience.

Perhaps the philosophical rationale for audience-determined news is the same one that has resulted in a shift in several areas from an emphasis on the press to an emphasis on the public. Examples: increasing talk about "public access to the media" and the "public's right to know." Now we have people talking about a kind of "public's right to determine what is news." Granted, the public (nonjournalists) can consider anything it desires to be news. As a member of the general public I have a right to determine what I want to call news; and I can pass this on to whomever I wish. But, in the context of *journalism* (or of the press) such determination is up to journalists, not members of the public.

Said another way, as a private citizen I have the right to make home movies and to show them to anyone who will watch. But I do not have a right to determine for a cinema owner or a television director that my home movies be shown in their facilities. In effect, I *can* indeed determine what I want to consider a "movie" but this does not, and should not, imply that I will determine what is to be shown as a movie through the mass media. This is the prerogative of the media decision makers. Market forces, of course, must be taken into consideration, for no medium of mass communication is an island. But news determination, like "movie" determination, lies with the disseminating medium.

Only a stupid or unrealistic editor would continue providing his readers with news which was not wanted nor read by these readers. In fact, the newspaper would not exist very long if this were done. So it can be assumed that, in the case of viable newspapers, the editors are taking the news values of the readers seriously. However, they are not being dictated to by the readers; they can, and do, often go against the wishes of the readers. Admittedly, many journalistic news-determiners do bow to the wishes of segments of their readership; this pandering often results in shallow and largely sensational material with negative overtones being the main news fare. Some editors do, indeed, stoop to the lowest common denominator.

But the question here is whether this *should* be the case? Should market forces determine the news? My answer is: No! An editor or any journalist responsible for news judgments should make news decisions. This is the nature of journalism. This is the responsibility and job for journalists as long as they, not nonjournalists, are in the business of news collection, definition, and dissemination.

FURTHER READING

Argyris, Chris. *Behind the Front Page: Organizational Self-renewal in a Metropolitan Newspaper* (San Francisco: Jossey-Bass, 1974).

Burgoon, Judee and Michael, and Charles Atkin. *What Is News? Who Decides? And How?* A report of the American Society of Newspaper Editors. Michigan State University, 1982.

DeFleur, Melvin L., and Everette E. Dennis. *Understanding Mass Communication* (Boston: Houghton Mifflin, 1981.)

Dennis, Everette E. *The Media Society: Evidence About Mass Communication in America* (Dubuque: W. C. Brown, 1978). See especially Part II, "Looking Inside: The Media's Social Institutions."

Gans, Herbert. *Deciding What's News* (New York: Pantheon, 1979).

Gitlin, Todd. *The Whole World Is Watching: Mass Media in the Making and Unmaking of the New Left* (Berkeley: University of California Press, 1980).

Sigal, Leon V. *Officials and Reporters: The Organization and Politics of Newsmaking* (Lexington, Mass.: D. C. Heath, 1973).

Thoreau, Henry David. *Walden, Or Life in the Woods* (Boston and New York: Houghton Mifflin, 1854).

Journalism as a Profession

11

Although there is a continuing debate over what constitutes a profession, there is widespread belief (especially among journalists) that journalism is a profession. There is a Society of Professional Journalists. Journalism is included in various standard listings of professions in America.

Even the most snobbish critics and scholars studying professional ethics include journalists in their discussions. Efforts to enhance the professionalization of journalists abound in seminars, workshops, codes of ethics, and other activities. Although it is said that freedom of the press, as guaranteed by the First Amendment, prohibits the control or licensing of journalists, newspapers still strive toward professionalism.

Clearly, journalists like to be associated with professionalism and they see no particular advantage in being members of a trade or a simple vocation. Professionalism is associated with competence, with training, with a body of knowledge, with standards of evaluation and improvement.

Is journalism a profession, then? If it is not, *should* it be? The debate goes on.

149

Merrill: Journalism is *not* a profession.

Contrary to traditional journalistic wisdom, journalism is not a profession. Perhaps "traditional" is the wrong word, for there really is not much tradition behind the idea of journalism being a profession. It is of recent vintage. For most of America's journalistic history, professionalism was no issue; if anybody thought of what journalism might be called at all, it was usually simply referred to as a trade, craft, or vocation.

Today the term and concept of *profession* has proliferated in journalistic rhetoric—in publications, speeches, and conversations. Journalists generally like to think of themselves as "professionals" and journalism as a "profession." I recently had a journalism student so emotionally tied to the idea that journalism is a profession that the very idea that it might not be distressed her greatly. "That's the reason I wanted to go into journalism—because it was a profession," she stated with apparent consternation.

Journalists seem to be impressed with the general esteem, respectability, and even awe that surrounds any organized activity carrying the name "profession." They have also observed that law and medicine, for instance, in being accepted as professions have taken on an elite image and that their practitioners are generally paid better than are most nonprofessionals.

It is understandable that journalists, often intellectuals or pseudointellectuals, find the lure of professionalism very strong. It would give them the aura of respectability, of public acceptance, of dignity, of exclusivity, and at least the collective psychological comfort denied them if they simply functioned as "journalists."

The notion that journalism is a profession is undoubtedly growing in America, but individual journalists do not really know what journalistic professionalism entails, what being a "professional" really means. Even two journalists with similar backgrounds may act in ways which each would consider "unprofessional." Even members of Sigma Delta Chi, the professional journalistic society, do not agree in many basic and important respects about journalism and its practices.

The observer looking at American journalism today can see very easily that journalists really do not have a single identity, nor do they share the same values, nor do they have a common definition of their role.

What, we should ask at this point, is a profession? Originally *profession* meant simply the act of professing; it has developed from that fundamental concept to mean, according to the *Oxford Snorter Dictionary*, the "occupation which one professes to be skilled in and to follow. . . . a vocation in which professed knowledge of some branch of learning is used in its application to the affairs of others, or in the practice of an art based upon it."

Even now, professionals profess; they profess to know better than others the nature of certain matters, and to know better than their nonprofessional clients what they need to know and in what proportion they need to know it. Professionals claim the exclusive right to practice, as a vocation, the arts that they profess to know.

William J. Goode, one of America's foremost sociologists, has insisted that professionals constitute a homogeneous community whose members share values, identity, and definition of role and interests. He has said that members of a profession "are bound by a sense of identity" and "share values in common."

The Bureau of Labor Statistics lists these requirements for a profession: (1) prescribed educational standards, (2) licensing, and (3) enforcement of performance standards by the profession itself.

Here are some other characteristics of a profession which are given in the influential book *The Professions in America:*

- A member of a profession is expected to think objectively and inquiringly about matters that may be, for the outsider, subject to "orthodoxy and sentiment which limit intellectual exploration." (Is this true for the journalist?)

- A member of a profession assumes that he can be trusted since he professes to have certain expertise that the layman does not have. (Can a journalist say this with justification?)

- A member of a profession believes in close solidarity with other members and thinks that it is a good thing to present a solid front to those outside the profession. (Is this true of a journalist?)

- A member of a profession is able to meet various minimum entrance standards for the profession—such as a degree in the professional area, a special license identifying him as a professional member in good standing, and so on. (Is this true of a journalist?)

- A member of a profession is not only certified or licensed but can

151

expect to be put out of the profession (in the case of a journalist—"depressed") if he does not live up to professional standards. (Is this true of a journalist?)

- A member of a profession has a code of ethics governing their activities in concert with other professionals and submits to a high degree of group control. (Is this true of a journalist?)

- A member of a profession participates in a system of rewards (monetary and honorary) for those who conduct themselves most notably within their code of ethics. (Is this true of the journalist?)

- A member of a profession shares in a discrete and substantive body of knowledge available to those in the profession. (Is this true of a journalist?)

After looking at some of the characteristics of a profession, as given above, we should ask: Is journalism a profession? Obviously it is not, although it has some of a profession's characteristics—or it approaches in some respects a profession. (A donkey, we might say, has many of the characteristics of a horse; it "approaches" a horse. But we must say quite definitely that it is not a horse.)

There is no direct relationship between journalists and their clients. A journalist is not a self-employed person; he works for an employer. There are, in journalism, no formal minimum entrance requirements; anyone can be a journalist who can get themselves hired—experience or no experience, degree or no degree. No journalist is expected (or required) to abide by any code of ethics. No journalist is certified or licensed—at least in the United States. No professional standards are commonly agreed upon, and followed, by journalists. A person working for the *National Enquirer* is just as much a journalist as a person working for the *New York Times*. A person writing news for the *Podunk Weekly Bugle* is just as much a journalist as a newsperson working for the *Wall Street Journal*.

Journalists do not share in common a "high degree of generalized and systematic knowledge." They do not claim the exclusive right to practice the arts (all borrowed from other disciplines) of their vocation. And finally, American journalists do not comprise "a homogeneous community."

Listen to a contemporary commentator, Irving Kristol, writing in 1972: "Even to speak of the 'profession' of journalism today is to indulge in flattering exaggeration. Journalism has not, as yet, acquired the simplest external signs of a profession" (Kristol, 1975, p. 26).

Even though journalism is not a profession, it *can* through increased stress on ethical codes, press councils, peer pressure, licensing of some kind, entrance requirements, and more rigorous standards for journalism education grow into a true profession. I don't contend that it is impossible for journalism to become a profession, just that it has not yet happened. What is more, I think that it *undesirable* that it evolves into a profession.

The philosopher William Barrett, writing about professions, states my feeling very well in these words:

> The price one pays for having a profession is a *déformation professionelle*, as the French put it—a professional deformation. Doctors and engineers tend to see things from the viewpoint of their own specialty, and usually show a very marked blind spot to whatever falls outside this particular province. The more specialized a vision the sharper its focus; but also the more nearly total the blind spot toward all things that lie on the periphery of this focus (Barrett, 1958, pp. 4–5).

There appears to be a deep-rooted desire among press people to belong to a select group (a "hierarchical longing within the press," as Lewis Lapham has called it in *Harper's*). It seems clear to me that this tendency, if carried very far, would stamp out unusual or eccentric concepts and, ultimately, also the journalists who embrace them. Lapham wrote that the more the press becomes a profession, the more it will "discourage the membership of rowdy amateurs" and, as it is with other professions, encourage the promotion of people who are "second-rate."

No doubt, professionalism will certainly restrict the ranks of journalism, eliminate the "nonprofessional" from practice, and the make the press appear more respectable—at least from the perspective of the elitists making up the profession.

In addition to a loss of diversity in journalism, another reason why journalism should not be a profession is one which has been put forward on numerous occasions by James W. Carey, dean of the College of Communications at the University of Illinois. It is that if journalism were a profession its practitioners would increasingly turn inward on themselves, thinking more and more about their own vested interests and mechanisms for self-protection, and less and less about their responsibilities to their audiences. Professions, believes Carey, tend to become ingrown and selfish with a kind of complacent and arrogant spirit contagious among their members.

I totally agree with Carey; it would be a pity if journalism, one of the most open, diversified institutions in the country—one that is largely dedicated to public service—were to change into a narrow, monolithic, self-centered professionalized fellowship devoid of an outward-looking and service orientation.

So, I maintain that journalism is not a profession and that it should not be one.

Dennis: Journalism *is* a profession.

Whether journalism is a profession is one of the oldest, continuing controversies in journalism. It used to be easier to take sides when the debate was simply whether journalism was a profession or a business. Liberals lined up on the side of professionalism while conservatives liked to see journalism as a profit-making enterprise. But those were simpler times. Today we can look back on a half century of striving by journalists and journalistic organizations to achieve professional status.

Journalism is commonly regarded as a profession made up of professional communicators, dedicated to professional standards. Journalists themselves believe this and even some of the most snobbish of American institutions engaged in the study of the professions consider journalists—warts and all—to be professionals. The Harvard-Hastings Program on Ethics in the Professions, for example, has no problem calling journalism a profession. Neither do such distinguished sociologists as Morris Janowitz or Herbert Gans who have contributed mightily to the literature of professionalism generally as well as journalism specifically.

Admittedly there are some scholars who quibble with this designation, preferring instead to call journalism a "subprofession." They would, no doubt, say that the terms *profession* and *professional* are too widely and indiscriminately used in America. The commonly understood definitions of *profession, professional,* and *professionalism* vary widely from those who say that a *profession* is simply a "principal calling, vocation, or employment" versus a more rigid view that insists a profession is "a calling requiring specialized knowledge and long, intensive preparation." (Both definitions are found in *Webster's Third New International Dictionary.*)

Most students of the sociology of work, concerned with professionalism, acknowledge that professions *evolve.* They are not created with all the finishing touches on Day One with their standards and practices intact. Medicine, for example, had little in the way of universal standards or educational requirements in this country until after 1915. Some commentators say that the law did not truly become a profession until the establishment of law schools.

Journalism has most, if not all, the distinctive marks of a profession and deserves to be so classified. This assertion is not just caving into popular parlance (as with "professional" actors or "professional" athletes), but because most of the major criteria that distinguish a profession from a trade or calling are integral to journalistic practice in America. What's more, dedication to professionalism is growing in journalism.

Like other professions, journalism has most of the characteristics of professionalism with different degrees of intensity. One of the primary marks of any profession (and not mentioned in the "Challenge") is "the kind of work that has for its prime purpose the rendering of a public service." Journalism is, in fact, engaged in a public service—the free flow of information and ideas is at the core of First Amendment freedom in the United States. The press has special protection under the Constitution, not simply to allow newspaper and broadcast owners to make a profit, but because as a matter of law and social policy we believe that a free press is essential to a functioning democracy. Of course the press must make a profit if it is to survive and reporters and editors have salaries and get various ego rewards for their work. Yet, most of them would contend (and with justification) that they render a public service. Certainly law, medicine, architecture, education, and the other professions engage in public service activity and still provide a living for their practitioners. That does not exclude them from the august company of professionals. Under the most rigid definition probably only the clergy—and then only the highly trained clergy— could qualify as professionals.

For purposes of this discussion, I accept the standards set out in *The Professions in America*, even though it presents a rather dated and stodgy view of professionalism. Does journalism qualify under this definition? I believe it does. Can a journalist "think objectively and inquiringly about matters" which by "sentiment and orthodoxy" limit outsiders? Certainly one of the purposes of journalism is to provide an impartial, disinterested synthesis of information. It identifies and explains conflicting viewpoints. This process helps the uninitiated understand what is happening in society without being subject to deliberate bias, or distortion. Journalism tells us that a "supply side" economist says one thing while a Keynesian says another.

Does a journalist have expertise a layman does not? Yes, of course. Journalists are experts at news gathering—searching out, assessing, and presenting information; is standard definitions of mass communication specify that "professional communicators," not amateurs, are required.

Does a journalist have "close solidarity" and "a solid front?" Not in the sense that medicine might, but that is because journalism is so diverse, involving many different kinds of media enterprises and professionals. Certainly journalists are organized through professional societies, guilds, unions, and other more specialized subgroups. I can think of few professionals with more solidarity than journalism when a fellow journalist is jailed or when a lively First Amendment issue emerges. Powerful publishers join with lowly reporters to fight a common battle. One of the clichés of the media when a story is attacked or seriously questioned is "We stand behind our reporter."

What of minimum entrance requirements? While there is no formal licensing, most media organizations do have minimum standards of education or experience before hiring anyone. They can deviate from these requirements if they wish, but rarely do. Increasingly journalists are graduates of professional schools of journalism accredited by a national body that is sanctioned by the government through the U.S. Office of Education. This procedure is not the same as licensing, but there are many other types of "conformity" and "sanctioning" within journalism. There is considerable agreement among journalists on a whole range of values and craft attitudes, as studies by communications researchers have shown. It is by no means an "every man an island" profession.

Can someone be "put out" of the profession? Not by the government, but certainly by the informal hiring practices of media organizations. Someone who consistently violates professional norms and standards or who is regarded as "sleazy" by his colleagues may have difficulty getting a job at a reputable publication. There may always be an outlet for that person's work, say in *The National Enquirer*, but not likely on the *Washington Post* or *New York Times*. After the celebrated Janet Cooke episode at the *Washington Post* in 1981, many media executives tightened up their hiring policies and developed clear standards. Increasingly, press councils, which make public pronouncements and have the power of embarrassment, provide a voluntary, policing function in journalism. Their work is advisory, but it does help guide performance.

Journalism has codes of ethics, as Chapter 12 in this book indicates. They help define professionalism and assist journalists with ethical dilemmas. On some papers a reporter who violates the code can be fired. In that instance, adherence to the code is a condition of employment. *The Editor & Publisher International Yearbook* lists several pages of awards, both financial and honorary, available to journalists. Some of the most prestigious, such as the Pulitzer Prizes and Nieman Fellowships can have a marked impact on their recipients' careers. These awards are given for exemplary performance.

The criteria of a "discrete and substantive body of knowledge" is more difficult. Because journalism is part of a system of freedom of expression, it is not possible nor desirable to prescribe just what every journalist must know. However, there is a standard curriculum in the journalism schools that includes courses in communication theory, media history, law, and ethics as well as other substantive topics. It is also generally agreed that journalists should be broadly educated in the liberal arts and sciences. In addition, professional schools have professional practice and skills courses in reporting, editing, photojournalism, and other topics. There is also a substantial literature of journalism, which includes both scholarly studies and such anecdotal materials as memoirs and media criticism. There are even subfields—journalism history, law, economics, theory and methodology, international communications, media sociology, and others. Each of these subfields has enough of a "corpus" of scholarship worthy of considerable attention by scholars. Journalism studies are also part of a larger literature of mass communication that has strong links to psychology, sociology, anthropology, and political science. Students of journalism have a rich lode to consider if they wish to master the field. Of course, there is no formal requirement that anyone do this.

More than half of all journalists in America are graduates of journalism schools and virtually all have at least a liberal arts education. Increasingly, some journalists have specialized education or training in such areas as science, law, politics, or the arts. Again the diversity of journalism in America makes the implementation of one single model of education or training impossible. Some professional communicators in broadcasting must hold Federally issued broadcast licenses attesting to certain technical competencies.

Fundamentally, journalists must know enough—gained either in formal education or on the job—to function in their work. If they do not, they are fired or otherwise excluded from the profession.

Just because all journalists do not march to the beat of a single drummer does not mean they are not professional. As Morris Janowitz has written

Practitioners in any particular profession hold differing conceptions of their tasks and priorities. The differences between the "public health" doctor and the clinician is a long-standing distinction that has had a strong impact on the practice of medicine. Since World War I, journalists have come more and more to consider themselves as professionals and to search for an appropriate professional model. The initial efforts were to fashion journalism into a field, similar to medicine, where the journalist would develop his technical expertise and also a sense of professional responsibility (Janowitz, 1975, p. 618).

That was the "gatekeeper" tradition which emphasized the search for objectivity, mentioned in Chapter 8. There are, as we have mentioned, other journalists who disagree with this view and instead say journalists should be advocates for causes and participate in public affairs. This conflict, according to sociologists John Johnstone, Edward Slawski, and William Bowman, that "would appear to pit proponents of a professionalized objective, restrained, and technically efficient journalism against those advocating a socially responsible journalism inspired by some of the same journalistic norms which were the objects of earlier reforms" (Johnstone et al., 1976, p. 523).

Is journalism a profession? The evidence is resounding. Sociological quibblers can find flaws in all of the professions that might put them outside of purist definitions, but this is not reality. Journalism is a profession not because its practitioners say they are professionals, but because it more than meets most of the criteria that, taken together, constitute a profession. And, as one wag, put it, "It looks like a profession, it sounds like a profession, it feels like a profession. Hell, it even smells like a profession!"

American Society Newspaper Editors. *What Is News? Who Decides? And How?* Preliminary Report on the World of the Working Journalist, American Society of Newspaper Editors, 1982. Also cited in earlier chapters as Burgoon et al. (1982).

Barrett, William. *Irrational Man: A Study in Existential Philosophy* (Garden City, N.Y.: Doubleday Anchor Books, 1958).

Birkhead, Douglas. "Presenting the Press: Journalism and the Professional Project" (Ph.D. dissertation, School of Journalism, University of Iowa, 1982).

Carey, James. "The Communications Revolution and the Professional Communicator," *Sociological Review* (University of Keele) 13 (1969).

Gerald, J. Edward. *The Social Responsibility of the Press* (Minneapolis: University of Minnesota Press, 1963).

Janowitz, Morris. "Professional Models in Journalism: The Gatekeeper and the Advocate," *Journalism Quarterly* 4 (Winter 1975) *52*, 618–626, 662.

Johnstone, John W. C., et al. *The Newspeople: A Sociological Portrait of American Journalists and Their Work* (Urbana: University of Illinois Press, 1976).

———, et al. "The Professional Values of American Newsmen," *Public Opinion Quarterly*, Vol. 36, No. 4, pp. 522–40.

Kristol, Irving. "Is the Press Misusing Its Growing Power," *More,* Jan. 1975, pp. 26–28.

Lynn, Kenneth S., ed. *The Professions in America* (Boston: Houghton Mifflin, 1965).

Public Agenda Foundation. *The Speaker and the Listener* (New York: The Foundation, 1980).

Southern Newspaper Publishers Association. *Education for Newspaper Journalists in the 1970s and Beyond* (Reston, Va. SNPA, 1973). See especially "Professionalism of the Press" by William E. Porter.

Press Councils
and Ethical Codes

12

Social responsibility has been a watchword for the press for many years. In recent times, the term "accountability" has also been added to discussions of journalistic practice. It is often agreed that mandatory controls to enforce press accountability would be inappropriate, but that various methods of self-regulation would be more acceptable.

Two such methods (or instruments of criticism) are the press council and the code of ethics.

Codes of ethics have been a part of American journalism for nearly 75 years. Many individual publications, trade associations, professional societies, and others have promulgated them and actively campaign for their use. Press councils are a more recent development in America—mainly since the late 1960s, although there were some important forerunners.

Press councils are private, voluntary organizations that appraise the performance of the press and other media, as well as adjudicating complaints short of actual legal sanctions. Press councils are often seen as safety valves, allowing the public to criticize press performance without formal or legal threats to the media. Ethical codes are more plentiful in America than are press councils, although both are frequently and vigorously discussed and debated. Both can be seen either as instruments for improvement of the press or as instruments for controlling the press and diminishing the potency and pluralism of the press. The debate goes on.

Merrill: Press councils and ethical codes are dangerous control mechanisms.

It is not popular to take the position that press councils and journalistic ethical codes are unnecessary at best and dangerous at worst. But that is the position I must take.

Councils and codes, and their popularity in many press quarters, evidence a symptom of journalistic defensiveness and insecurity that has grown with mounting lay sophistication in the field of communication and in the face of growing public hostility and criticism of the mass media.

One way to try to head off or diminish this flood of criticism and abuse—certainly this wave of growing skepticism about the press—is for the press to try to do a better job of policing itself. At least the press must make the public *believe* it is trying to clean up its own act. Thus increased emphasis on press councils and codes of ethics, two of the most obvious of the policing mechanisms.

Certainly there is good reason for the press to be concerned with its public image. Press performance is certainly no more commendable and ethical than the performance of other public institutions so often called to task by the press. A former newspaper editor in Detroit has put it harshly in these words.

> There are good men and women who will not stand for office, concerned that you [the press] will find their flaws or invent them. Many people who have dealt with you wish that they had not. You are capricious and unpredictable, you are fearsome and you are feared, because there is never any way to know whether this time you will be fair and accurate or whether you will not. And there is virtually nothing we can do about it (Luedtke, 1982, p. 16).

It is widely believed that the press itself should do something about such problems. So we put more and more faith in councils and codes. There seems to be a deep-seated fear in the press that one of these days the people are going to get fed up with journalistic excesses and arrogance and the walls of old concepts of press freedom will come tumbling down.

With councils and codes, the press is trying to put a little mortar in the cracks that are appearing in the traditional walls. What I maintain is that these councils and codes have the potential of harming freedom and pluralism as much, if not more, than the criticism which might come from the public. It is not to councils and codes that the press must trust for ethical practice and more public responsibility: Individual journalists must determine to be more ethical and more truly concerned with the excesses and shady actions of their daily work.

In 1981 alone there were some well-publicized instances of journalistic wrongdoing. A columnist for the New York *Daily News* had to resign when he was accused of making up a story about a clash between a gang of youths in Belfast and a British military patrol. A *Washington Post* reporter was forced to resign and surrender her Pulitzer Prize when it turned out that her heroin addict story was pure fiction. A reporter for the *Toronto Sun* was fired and another had to resign when they had no documentation for a story implicating a Cabinet member in stock manipulations.

Activities of this magnitude may, as it is often said by journalists, be exceptions and have been overemphasized. But certainly there are innumerable instances of malpractice in journalism—the great majority of them never getting any public exposure. Since public exposures of atypical and unusual malpractices in other social organizations are regular grist for the journalistic mills, it should be easy for the press to understand public interest in the press's own derelictions, however infrequent.

The idea of news councils is not new, although the rhetoric surrounding them has escalated greatly in the past few years. The first press council was established in Sweden more than a half century ago. Today there are some 30 press councils in the world. Some are government-connected and some are run exclusively by the press itself. Some, like the U.S.'s National News Council, have press and lay members. Typical of this last type is the British Press Council (created in 1953 and revised in 1963). The basic purpose of such bodies is to investigate and rule on public complaints against the press so as to make the press more responsible and to avoid restrictive government regulation.

In the United States, the National News Council was formed in 1972. Various state councils—e.g., in Minnesota and Hawaii—and local councils—e.g., Redwood City and Santa Rosa in California—were also founded. All news councils in America have been controversial. Many editors and journalists oppose the whole concept of news councils as a possible first step toward government regulation.

There are nations that, through their press councils, exercise control over the press, issue (and revoke) journalistic licenses, and impose jail sentences on reporters as well as levy fines on newspapers.

The *New York Times* has never supported the National News Council in the United States. Its publisher has said that the newspaper wants nothing to do with it, that the *Times* already has its "council"— its subscribers. The executive editor of the *Times*, A. M. Rosenthal, has pointed out that peer pressure can lead to a kind of regulation or control just as can regulatory pressure from government or some outside entity.

I feel that the *New York Times* is correct in arguing that the Council is unnecessary and even dangerous. Its attitude toward the Council has meant that other newspapers have had support for their doubts about the Council. It helps to be in the company of such a well-known and highly respected newspaper as the *Times*. So, now, the "bottom line"—as the saying goes—is that the National News Council, while continuing its work, is not really taken seriously by anyone except, perhaps, its own members.

Proponents of news councils feel that the press needs to be criticized, to have its work observed and commented upon regularly. And, they say, this is the purpose of a news council; it is not designed to coerce, and its pressure is only the pressure of publicity. This, they contend, poses no real danger to press freedom.

Nevertheless, the Council's existence has not in any notable way improved American journalism. It, like the press itself, has credibility problems—and perhaps will as long as it selects its own members and can be accused of "stacking" its ranks with media people. Also when some group like the News Council constantly presumes to define for the press what "good practice" and proper ethical behavior are, there is the danger of pushing the press in the direction of a monolithic conformity which is traditionally anathema to a libertarian journalistic system.

Back in 1973, Clayton Kirkpatrick, editor of the *Chicago Tribune,* stated that the price for press councils was simply too high and the evidence that they were needed was "too subjective." He believed, as I do, that inevitably press councils must set up universal standards, and that these will lead to conformity. "Out go the rebels, the undergrounders, the angry, daring, and uncouth," he wrote. "America," he said, "would be poorer for that. Maybe the press would be more respectable, but not so exciting or effective." (Kirkpatrick, 1973, p. 33).

And listen to Arthur Ochs Sulzberger, publisher of the *New York Times,* writing in the journal just quoted:

> Just as we believe that the Council will not be of help, we believe that it could do much harm. In sitting in judgment on the accuracy and fairness of news reporting, the Council will have to devise standards against which to make determinations. We do not think this is possible to do or advisable to try. . . . What is right for *The Times* and its News Service may not be for a wire service or a television network or a magazine. We do not wish anyone to impose standards on us (Sulzberger, 1973, p. 34).

So, in concluding these remarks about press councils and about the National News Council in particular, I would say that all this talk of "press responsibility" subordinates press freedom and journalistic diversity and gives an ominous clue to the priorities of any press council.

And, now, to Codes of Ethics.

The dangers I see implicit in news councils can be projected to ethical codes also. There is an implicit "conformity desire" in codes as in news councils. Somebody or some group is setting itself up as an arbiter of media conduct—and this in a system which is theoretically pluralistic and self-determining. Although codes of journalistic ethics have considerable support among media people, many journalists insist that a code is useless because it cannot cover all the problems which a journalist will encounter. Actually, they say, each journalist must make ethical decisions for himself and cannot—and should not—be hemmed in and directed by some code devised by someone else.

Many journalistic groups and organizations, however, do have codes of ethics—e.g., CBS and NBC, the American Society of Newspaper Editors, and the Society of Professional Journalists, Sigma Delta Chi. Some newspapers have their own ethical codes; others do not. "Most codes are just a bunch of platitudes," says William Thomas, editor of the *Los Angeles Times*. In blunt language he continues, "I've never seen a written code of ethics that wasn't so damned obvious that it was clear that you were doing it more for its outside PR (public relations) value than for any inward impact."

Let us look for a moment at the Code of Ethics of Sigma Delta Chi, the Society of Professional Journalists. It is a good example of what is wrong with ethical codes. In 1973 the code, an updated version of an older 1926 version, was adopted to make it a stronger statement.

The Code of Ethics, written by a committee chaired by Casey Bukro of the *Chicago Tribune*, is a loosely and vaguely written document, filled with generalizations and semantically foggy clichés. Such phrases stating that SDXers believe in "public enlightenment as the forerunner of justice," "obligations that require journalists to perform with intelligence, objectivity, accuracy, and fairness," and "serving the general welfare" are sprinkled throughout the code. We are told that journalists uphold the right to speak unpopular opinions and that journalists must have no obligation to any interest except the public's right to know the truth.

We are given the usual litany of don'ts—not taking gifts, free trips, special treatment, and secondary employment. And on and on goes the code, setting up guidelines for members of the society—and for all journalists. Numerous meaningless pronouncements and directions are given, and at the end of the code journalists are directed to "actively censure and try to prevent violations of these standards" and "to encourage their observance by all newspeople." So at the end we learn that this code is not just a control mechanism for members of SDX but for "all newspeople."

For more specific criticism of the SDX Code of Ethics, the reader is invited to *Existential Journalism*, pp. 130–132, and to my chapter "Rhetoric" in *Philosophy and Journalism* (1983). It is enough here simply to say that the careful reader of the Code (and all journalistic codes) will recognize the uselessness of such codes—while at the same time understanding the potential danger they could inflict on freedom and diversity if taken seriously. Fortunately, such codes are not taken seriously; this is their redeeming feature, in my opinion.

In conclusion, let me reiterate: Press councils and journalistic codes of ethics are dangerous control mechanisms that stand alluringly at the door of American journalism waiting to be let in and welcomed. Seductive though they may be to a journalistic world often looking for redemption from a multitude of actual and assumed transgressions, they should be banished lest they get into the Journalistic House of Freedom and contaminate it in the name of journalistic responsibility.

Dennis: Press councils and ethical codes are useful instruments of criticism that can improve the media.

Professor Merrill argues quite convincingly that press councils and ethical codes are superfluous, self-serving, and even dangerous. This purist position almost instantly conjures up an image of crazed Naderesque crusaders who would shackle the press and emasculate freedom through a system of constraining rules. But, a look at the real world gives us a quite different view.

Those who promulgated codes and organized press councils were not activists with Draconian values, but sensitive media professionals and public-spirited citizens who want a strong, free press that is ethical and competent in its performance. This is not a lofty ideal, but a belief that the press can be improved if there are formal channels for public comment and criticism and if professionals have standards against which they can make individual decisions. And notably, no one is imposing anything since both press councils and codes of ethics are *voluntary*. They have only an advisory function; they make suggestions; they are not the rule of law; if they have any power it is only the "power of embarrassment." They can point to poor practices or praise good ones. In fact, they are preventive mechanisms that can head off legal sanctions and heavy penalties. For example, most press councils require those bringing grievances to waive their right to sue later on.

"Ethics," as Professor Merrill has pointed out in *The Imperative of Freedom*, "is that branch of philosophy that helps journalists determine what is right to do in their journalism; it is very much a normative science of conduct, with conduct considered primarily as self-determined voluntary conduct" (Merrill, 1974, p. 165). Later in the same book he asks whether ethics should be "individualistic" or "group-approved." Not surprisingly, he prefers the individual choice to that of group norms. I do not think the two need to be mutually exclusive. One can have codes of ethics and press council proceedings that become a kind of "common law" of media ethics against which individuals can exercise their minds and good judgment with regard to individual cases. That is as it should be.

In fact, Professor Louis Hodges of Washington and Lee University makes this point when he says the real value of ethical codes may not be so much in the finished product—the code itself—as in the *process* that professionals go through in writing codes. "I'd have everyone write a code; then throw it away," says Hodges. Those who participated would learn from the experience. In Hodges's ideal situation all media professionals would engage in the code-making process. In reality, of course, this is not likely to occur. Therefore, codes of ethics fashioned by journalists for journalists are the next best thing. Codes set standards and help distinguish virtuous practices that serve the public interest from those that do not. They would enhance the position of the press in society by seeing that it is truly independent, free, and responsible.

Codes of ethics developed by professional societies or editors' associations are general philosophical statements that promote impartiality, fair play, and decency. Codes formulated by individual news organizations are usually much more specific. They have rules on such matters as gifts, outside employment, conflicts of interest, advocacy, accuracy, and plagiarism, among others. In some instances, these guidelines become conditions of employment, but exceptions and waivers are always possible. Who is to say that it is not all right for a newspaper or television station to tell its employees that they do not want them accepting "freebies" such as trips, tickets, or other gifts? Or that they should not misrepresent themselves or plagiarize material from other sources? Such standards spelled out in codes enhance the credibility of journalism and give the audience more confidence in the news. Of course, ethical codes are mostly insider's rules and not widely publicized.

By contrast, press councils are more public. To begin with they are private, voluntary organizations which are usually (in America, at least) made up of a mix of media people and public members. The public members represent such interests as education, business, labor, minorities, and religion. A press council is a channel where public complaints about the media can be aired. Thus, the citizen has a neutral forum to raise questions about media performance. Press councils have no power of enforcement; they issue opinions and no one is obliged to accept them. In fact, far from being dangerous, press councils are most often criticized for being ineffective. I personally do not think this is necessarily the case, as I will point out later. What press councils do is encourage healthy, public discussion to the mutual benefit of media and public.

While the discussion of press councils and ethics codes is nothing new, this debate had added urgency in the 1980s because of strong public dissatisfaction with the press. This is important because the media exist in society with many competing forces and organizations. Media need not be popular, but they must inspire enough public confidence to carry out their necessary information and opinion functions.

Thus, it is disturbing when pollsters report that the media face deepening public distrust. It is as though the individual citizen, like Paddy Chayefsky's deranged anchorman in *Network*, is saying, "I'm mad as hell and I'm not going to take it anymore!" In a 1982 survey ABC News reported that six of of every ten Americans favored a law that would prevent TV reporters from questioning people who do not want to be interviewed. Personal privacy, the respondents said, is more important than freedom of the press. A poll conducted by the *Los Angeles Times* found that only one person in three believes that news reporters are fair. A Gallup study revealed that the public ranks the honesty and ethics of reporters considerably below that of policy officers and just above that of business tycoons. Elsewhere in this book we mention studies by the Public Agenda Foundation that say the public believes that the media constrain individual freedom of expression by noncoverage or denial of access to divergent views. Similarly, a study by the American Society of Newspaper Editors shows that media professionals have a contemptuous view of their audience. These are not good signs. Personally, I believe that most of these assessments are patently unfair. Most journalists are scrupulously honest and their organizations take precautions to ensure fairness. The degree of professionalism in the media is stronger than ever. Yet few people know this and the media do little to let the public in on the secret.

The rights of a free press ultimately depend on the consent of citizens. Television and other media, says George Watson of ABC News "cannot protect that freedom simply by invoking the First Amendment. It needs to debate its rights and responsibilities and that demands a great effort to provide an attentive ear and open mind to the public's concern and criticism" ("TV Hear Viewers," 1982, p. A23).

One of the reasons we have this deplorable situation whereby the public gives the media such low marks is that we have so few channels for feedback, so little opportunity for criticism. There are very few press councils, and codes of ethics exist mostly in professional organizations and media industry groups. A relatively small number of individual news organizations have their own. Both codes and

169

councils are the exception in America, not the rule. Ethics codes are not particularly controversial, but press councils are. I believe this is because they are poorly understood.

Press councils are not ancient star chamber tribunals. They are settings for rationale debate and their findings are usually publicized in the press. For more than ten years, I was able to observe at close range the Minnesota News Council. More than anything else, the Minnesota Council was the conscience of journalism in that state. I saw complaints that questioned fairness in news coverage, the presentation of poll data, reporter interference with pending criminal investigations, and many more. One notable grievance from a defeated candidate for governor led to a lively discussion of how campaign issues are determined. In several instances, news organizations drafted new rules and policies for their staffs as a result of council findings. In other cases (about half, I believe) the council tilted toward the press and pointed up misunderstandings in the complaint. In short, the process was healthy. Charles W. Bailey, editor of the *Minneapolis Star and Tribune*, himself a somewhat reluctant convert to the press council idea stated publicly that the council had a strong, positive influence on his paper and on journalism in the state generally. As Bailey put it:

> In a society where the government cannot regulate the press—and that prohibition, though periodically dented by the courts, has so far fortunately been preserved—it is healthy to have some noncoersive device to monitor the performance of so powerful a societal institution (Bailey, Minnesota News Council brochure, undated)

A. H. Raskin of the *New York Times*, who has worked closely with the National News Council, agrees. "Of all the institutions of an increasingly complicated society, none is so addicted to self-righteousness, self-satisfaction and self-congratulation as the press" (Raskin, Minnesota News Council brochure). Press councils, he adds, provide an important check for the public.

One knowledgeable observer, Cameron Blodgett, executive director of the Minnesota News Council, argues vehemently in favor of councils because, he says, they can:

• Validate news media coverage.

- Reduce the number and costs of libel suits and complaints to the Federal Communications Commission.
- Provide audience feedback ... and point up public perceptions and misperceptions.
- Enhance credibility.
- Educate the public about how the media work.
- Preserve media freedom through a fair and effective press.
- Improve media performance and set standards of competence.

Adds Blodgett, "Press councils will not censor, fine, or regulate, nor will they result in government control."

Have press councils and ethical codes brought any notable improvement to the press in America? Perhaps they have not had a profound impact, but I would argue that is because there are relatively few councils. In the several local communities that experimented with press councils in the 1960s, Professor William L. Rivers and several colleagues in a notable study, *Backtalk: Press Councils in America* (New York: Canfield Press, 1971) reported that local community councils were generally effective. We have already cited the case of the Minnesota press council which is documented in detail by Robert Schafer in a master's thesis. The National News Council has had some modest impact, but its mandate is large and its resources quite modest. It would seem that press councils work best at the state and local levels.

The impact of ethical codes is difficult to measure. Most historians of the press, though, would agree that the performance of the press has improved markedly since the wide acceptance of social responsibility theory which is linked to the development of ethical codes. Certainly the press is enormously more professional and more responsible today than it was in the 1920s. I suspect that ethical codes have played some small part in this transformation in concert with journalism education, media criticism, growing professionalism, and other forces. They are interrelated and difficult to separate. Certainly, there are notable examples at particular American newspapers—the *Louisville Courier Journal* and *Milwaukee Journal* are among them—where strong ethics codes are proudly mentioned by staff members as a rationale for particular processes.

Critics of press councils and codes fear that they will become

171

stalking horses for those who would limit press freedom or push for government controls, but this is not the case. In fact, there are instances where newspapers, locked in litigation with angry defendants, cite codes of ethics to justify what they have done as standard journalistic practice. Such an instance arose in the case of Rebozo v. *The Washington Post* in 1982. As a part of the discovery process, lawyers for the *Post* stipulated that the newspaper subscribed to the American Society of Newspaper Editors Code of Ethics.

While codes and councils may not have had a profound and powerful influence to date, they are positive forces that benefit both the press and the public and they should be encouraged in every way possible. The maturation of a profession is measured in its ability to encourage and cope with criticism. Journalism is on its way thanks to councils and codes.

Space limitations here make it difficult to put the media code/council discussion in the context of codes of ethics and various enforcement procedures that are commonplace in the medical and legal professions, for example. Codes are usually promulgated to protect the profession, the individuals in it, and the consumers of services. Medical and legal codes of ethics are much better known to the general public than are those used by the media. The essential difference is that both medicine and law are licensed by the state and serious violations of ethics can be brought to the attention of licensing authorities or can be the basis for malpractice suits. In these instances, the code—and the council that is related to its enforcement—have actual power to strip a physician or lawyer of the right to practice. In journalism, all ethical codes are voluntary and there is no legal enforcement procedure that can be invoked.

FURTHER READING

Balk, Alfred. *A Free and Responsive Press* (New York: Twentieth Century Fund, 1973).

Hulteng, John L. *The Messenger's Motives* (Englewood Cliffs, N.J.: Prentice-Hall, 1976).

Merrill, J. C. *The Imperative of Freedom* (New York: Hastings House, 1974).

Merrill, J. C., and Ralph D. Barney, eds. *Ethics and the Press* (New York: Hastings House, 1975).

Murray, George, *The Press and the Public* (Carbondale: Southern Illinois University Press, 1972).

National News Council. *In the Public Interest, 1973–75* (New York, 1975).

Rivers, William L. *Back Talk: Press Councils in America* (San Francisco: Canfield Press, 1973).

Schafer, Robert. *The Minnesota News Council, A Ten Year Study* (M.A. Thesis, University of Minnesota, 1982).

"TV Hears Viewers," *New York Times* (August 25, 1982), p. A23.

Western Communications Imperialism

13

The idea that the mass media of communication are essentially "Western" (economically affluent and well-developed) in their orientation and that they promote Western values in the Third World (developing, poorer areas) and elsewhere is frequently discussed. So engrained is this idea that the term "communications imperialism," a pejorative notion on its face, is seldom debated any more.

This idea has been extended in recent years in discussions of the New International Information Order, a complex concept but with a central idea that the news flows from large nations to small ones with the larger nations' views predominating.

A UNESCO Commission headed by Sean MacBride has offered proposals that would give Third World nations more control over the news that flows out of their countries. This movement has resulted in cries of "censorship" and "news control" from the Western industrial nations.

A standard view is that the United States, in particular, extends its sphere into the Third World by its control of news agencies which use Western industrial standards in sorting out and deciding on the news. Communications imperialism is closely connected to the notion that information is power and that information is a renewable resource largely control from and by the West. Major perspectives in this controversy are presented below.

Merrill: The U.S. is *not* guilty of communications imperialism.

Communication imperialism is a harsh term. It is also an unfair one in the context of the debate now going on between the Third World (developing countries) and the First World (the "West" and the economically developed countries). The indictment of the West by the Third World (and the Second—Communist—world) implies *forced* projection of communications power into the Third World. It implies subservience by the Third World to the West through its "communications imperialism." It implies that the West *wants to* destroy national cultures and to bring the rest of the world under its cultural (and economic and political) hegemony. It implies that the nations of the world accepting media messages from the West are being forced to accept them, and that their own communications-determination is impotent.

These implications simply cannot be sustained by evidence. Western communications *influence* is undeniable throughout the world. To say that Arab oil influence is a fact in the world is quite different from saying that the Arabs are guilty of "oil imperialism."

Third World journalists and communications specialists increasingly are convinced that the developed countries dominate (and do not merely "influence") the communications systems of the developing world. Although some Third World spokesmen have talked of a cultural and communications "disassociation" from the major powers—a kind of boycott—most of them see this isolation as unrealistic since the big Western powers—especially the United States—have a virtual monopoly on world information. And through this world information monopoly, the West, they claim, is practicing *imperialism.*

In all the recent concern about a so-called New International Information Order, sparked by UNESCO, the fact that the West dominates the world news flow is perhaps the most frequent indictment. A Kenyan editor sums up the Third World's feeling about this: "Third World people have come to feel a great sense of impotence over the cultural influences which permeate their relations with the Western world throughout the mass media. It is an unrelenting one-way flow of ideas from Western countries to the Third World, with little opportunity given to the Third World nations to examine the content of the materials which daily flood their own presses." (Quoted in Richstad and Anderson, 1981, p. 61).

Typical of those critics who accuse the West is Luis Ramiro Beltran of Bolivia, a newspaperman and researcher.

"When the culture of a central and dominant country," he writes, speaking of the United States, "is *unilaterally imposed* over the peripheral countries it dominates *at the expense of their cultural integrity*, then the case is one of cultural imperialism." Beltran is referring to the U.S. and Latin America in this statement, but he and others maintain this "imperialism" is operative worldwide.

Listen to another prominent critic—Mustapha Masmoudi, Tunisia's permanent delegate to UNESCO, dealing with this subject:

> In addition to dominating and manipulating the international news flow, the developed countries practice other forms of hegemony over the communications institutions of the Third World. . . . advertising, magazines, and television programs are today so many instruments of cultural domination and accultura-tion, transmitting to the developing countries messages which are harmful to their cultures, contrary to their values, and detrimental to their development aims and efforts (Quoted in Richstad and Anderson, 1981, p. 81).

Masmoudi and others of the Third World have said that a small elite group in the West—especially the Western international news agen-cies—dominate and manipulate (or seek to) the world through their messages. The managing director of Britain's Reuters Ltd., one of the big agencies so indicted, has not taken this "communications imperial-ism" charge with as much patience as have other Western spokesmen. In an impromptu talk in Greece in 1979, Gerald Long blasted UNESCO for fostering such ideas:

> We have the Unesco Director General in 1977 saying that communication often appears as the privilege of a tightly knit group of professionals or technocrats who hold populations, so to speak, at their mercy and can direct, if not manipulate, them at will.
>
> This is nonsense. I would be very interested to see some support given by Unesco to the very wide-ranging and high-sounding affirmations that are made and for which no example whatsoever is adduced. I would like the Director-General to tell us

how the manipulation is brought about, how it works, to give us some examples of it. I know none" (Quoted in Richstad and Anderson, 1981, p. 275).

The Third World countries are understandably sensitive about the advanced nations' domination of the productive capacities for communications content and the technology of distribution. This domination has not happened in the field of communication alone, but in many fields of production and distribution; it is a fact of life in the world today that the more advanced technological nations dominate technologically. And this certainly applies to the area of communications. To deny technological dominance would be the height of naivete. But possession of an admirably advanced technology is something quite different from "imperialism," with its considerable negative overtones.

The tragedy today is that the West is such an easy target. Advanced Communist nations—the Second World—and the developing countries of the Third World have usurped the negative terms for use against the West. Third Worlders are the people in the White Hats; the Westerners are the bad boys of the world communications scene; the West exploits the Third World; the Second World, on the other hand, understands and loves the Third World. The West contributes to racism, nationalism, imperialism, and international friction.

Communist nations, especially the USSR, have convinced the Third World that the West is involved in cultural and communications imperialism. How can the Communist nations be imperialistic? After all, they have appropriated that term for use in referring to the West. They use it in concert with their ideological use of the term "political right"; the world's mind-set by now has it that the "left" cannot be imperialistic. How, the question goes, can Cuban forces fighting half way around the world be imperialistic? Are they not on "the left"? How can Soviet troops entering Afghanistan be imperialistic? How can they be charged with cultural, communication or any other kind of imperialism? Are they not simply "progressives of the left" who are engaged in "freeing" the "enslaved" people against whom they are fighting? Such is the semantic game.

For at least the last 15 years (and probably since World War II) the Communist propaganda machine has been tireless in its efforts to hide the true nature of the Second World and paint the West as evil. Buried under a barrage of misleading words and labels which Daniel Moynihan has called "semantic infiltration," countless millions of people—

largely in the developing Third World—have swallowed the semantic line, among others, that the West is guilty of communications imperialism. How, then, can people of the Third World be expected to take issue with the Second World which they have been taught is the enemy of this "Western communications imperialism"? Like most people, they seldom look behind the words and labels at the reality.

If Western communications specialists and scholars continue to permit the Second World to choose the words and labels by which the international communications dialogue is carried on, then the West will continue to lose the semantic battle. We cannot really expect the Second and Third Worlds to cease a semantic offensive which is proving so successful, but we can hope that the West will get into the fray and neutralize the effects of the verbal barrage.

Look for a moment at the word *imperialism*. It is unique in its capacity to make the Third World's political blood boil. Its stench is like that of the word *racist* among blacks. It hits people in the gut, as well as in the intellect. So the ideologues of the Second (Communist) World have expanded the use of the term beyond its basic political context and have tacked it onto the term *communications,* thereby lobbing a powerful bomb into the midst of Western journalism and communication. Not only now is the West politically imperialistic, but it is engaging, they say, in communications imperialism. They have co-opted another effective term. Also, by attaching it to the West, they have directed the term away from themselves, leaving them free of the onus of "imperialism."

Of course, many persons in academe and among the foreign affairs elite, and certainly among the communications specialists of the world, will condemn any Western attempt to neutralize the anti-Western semantic barrage as dangerous to world understanding and disruptive of "detente." One wonders why they do not say this about the one-sided semantic defamation which constantly pours from Second and Third World word arenals through the barrels of UNESCO's big guns to explode on Western sensitivities? We must stop taking it, stop being the "good guys" that can tolerate such semantic dishonesty. We should repudiate such terms applied to us—such terms as "communications imperialism." We urgently need—especially those of us concerned with communication—a greater semantic sophistication.

In the United States, Herbert Schiller and a few others have played fast and loose with the term "imperialism" as applied to American communications agencies and to American economic enterprises. The

American system generally is pictured as "imperialistic," presumably *forcing* its alien factories, products, news services, and messages on staunchly resisting foreign natives. This assertion is simply false.

The elites in most of the Third World condemn the U. S. for situations they refuse to face and try to solve themselves. Most of them have settled into their comfortable little niches, closing their eyes to the political corruption, secrecy, and passivity of their own nations; and from these complacent little niches they continue to wring their hands in journals, speeches, and in UNESCO forums about what the West is doing to them.

Jean-Francois Revel has put it nicely in writing about Latin American elites: they have carried "to an extreme a defect that is fatal to a society no less than to an individual: namely, the notion that everything bad that happens is never the fault of oneself, but always the fault of others" (Revel, 1979). This seems to describe exactly the journalistic situation in most Third World countries.

Many times I have heard editors and other journalists in the developing world indict American news agencies for not sending enough serious "developmental" stories to the Third World, for being concerned mainly with the more sensational and "negative" aspects of the news, and generally for participating in "communications im- perialism." Then, when the formality of our conferences was ended, I have accompanied them to their newspaper offices. What did I find there? They themselves were choosing and playing up the nonserious, sensational news items and throwing the serious stories into the wastebasket (and there were plenty of important stories). They themselves showed no real dedication to using "developmental" news—even that coming from their own reporters about their own countries or from neighboring Third World countries. And they themselves were often choosing AP and UPI stories for use and ignoring many other stories—many local and "positive" ones—which were available for use. Is this *imperialism* on the part of the West? I think not.

The American news agencies were not forcing these Third World journalists to use their material; American journalism was not coercing these newspapes to resemble in many respects American newspapers. This was a voluntary action on the part of the Third World journalists. There were alternatives—such as TASS and an assortment of national news agencies from the Third World itself. And there was always the possibility of rerunning stories (with or without rewriting them) from other Third World publications.

But generally the Third World editors eagerly will take from the wire the American stories, all the while (in conferences and articles) smearing the U.S. news agencies as inadequate and distorted. It is strange, indeed, that we hear so little criticism from them of the Communist agencies—especially TASS. What about the "unbiased and balanced" nature of the news distributed by these agencies? A very large number of Third World newspapers get reams of copy from TASS and from various Communist embassies in the country. They use practically none of it. Why? If the American-distributed news is so sensational, unrealistic, distorted, and negative, why not use more of the government-supportive and positive (almost puritanically so) news from TASS? It is difficult to get a straight answer to this question, but it seems that down deep these editors know which is the most newsworthy, believable, and interesting. *They*—the editors—in short, make the decision as to what their readers will read—not the American news agencies.

So it might be said—but usually is not—that the Third World journalists themselves are responsible for the biased pictures of the Third World—if, in fact, their common criticism is valid. Or, at least, they can be said to be major collaborators in such an unrealistic presentation. But the Third World journalists refuse to accept such a responsibility; they prefer instead to fault somebody else for their kind of journalism.

Little wonder most Third World journalistic systems are considered underdeveloped. And, undoubtedly they will remain so until they take a look at their own activities—at their own restrictive governments, at their own acceptance of certain definitions of news, at their own love for sensational news, at their own lapses in integrity in handing news, and at their own unwillingness to do their own share in working toward a better "balance" in the news flow.

Their continued paranoid rhetoric in world forums and their continued unconcern with their own actions in these criticized areas are seriously impeding progress toward more authentic and highly developed press systems in their countries. This points up the fatal flaw in the Third World's indictment of the West—and not only the area of communications imperialism: it evidences a continued unwillingness to accept responsibility for their *own* journalistic weaknesses.

It evidences, too, the fact that they refuse to admit that they *voluntarily* accept Western messages into their countries. Only when they are willing to do what they can to better the situation, to develop self-assurance and confidence necessary for real development and progress, will their communications situation change significantly. It takes real courage to do this, and so far there appear few signs of such courage emanating from either governmental leaders or communications specialists of the Third World.

Dennis: The U.S. *is* guilty of communications imperialism.

Although it is true that the term *imperialism* is an unfortunate one, it does refer to a real dilemma that pits Western nations against those of the Third World. It is said that media imperialism results in cultural imperialism and implants Western ideas and values, thus upsetting natural, evolutionary development. At its core, this argument is ideological. Those on the Left decry the existence and impact of cultural imperialism and those on the Right defend the contributions of Western communications enterprises in developing countries.

The rhetoric at international conferences on communications imperialism and the New World Information Order has been so contentious in recent years that little in the way of rational explanation emerges. Polemicists scream at other poemicists and the result is an unyielding atmosphere of mutual distrust and conflicting values.

The essence of the cultural-communications imperialism conflict is seen most vividly in examples:

A few years ago Ethiopian Radio imported dramatic programs from the United States. Around the time of the Christmas season, these programs promoted the European and American tradition of Christmas trees and gift giving. Ethiopia is a Coptic Christian country, where Christmas was strictly a religious holiday. However, the American programming led to a demand for Christmas trees and gift giving, in what can be seen as an unfortunate intrusion on local culture and customs. The trees had to be shipped in from the U.S.! This, says one critic, was media-induced cultural imperialism that had a direct effect on people's behavior.

Another Third World commentator says, "We are encouraged to buy Crest and brush our teeth three times a day when we don't have enough to eat." A number of scholars have recorded the extent of U.S.-produced content of mass media in other countries. In the case of television, a large number of countries and a strong majority of Third World nations use more than 60 percent of U.S. programs on their local channels. For example, I have seen "Gunsmoke" reruns in West Africa with Marshall Dillon and Miss Kitty speaking Igbo and heard "Wonder Woman" speaking Spanish in Mexico. What does it mean when so much of the television programming available to people in the

Third World comes from the U.S.? What impact does it have on their expectations when they get a glimpse of Western life styles on the screen? Will it foster revolution and unrest? How will hair styles, clothing, and other fads and fashions be influenced? What will be the effects of Western media content on individual behavior—or on the society and culture itself? Will there be a typically local adaptation or will Western media content upset natural cultural patterns and the lives of unsuspecting viewers who only know that they "want television"?

The reasons for the dominance of American content are obvious. We produce more programming and make it available more economically than any other nation in the world. Naturally, we are the primary supplier. Some people say that in time all countries will create their own software and programs. But the impact in the intervening years may be profound. Unfortunately there is little research on questions of impact, effects, and influence, so we are left with much speculation.

I believe that media imperialism is a reality even though it may not be the result of any kind of nefarious cabal by the Western powers as some Leftists argue. It occurred as a natural consequence of Western expansion that was done for the economic advantage of the West, not that of Third World nations. The continued dominance of Western communications enterprises and technology in the Third World is linked both to economic and to political interests that have great benefits for the U.S., Britain, France, and other countries in the West. If much of the direct daily impact of this activity is not caused by malevolent planning, the planning is at least insensitive.

As we have pointed out repeatedly in this book, we live in an information society. The world has passed from its agrarian and industrial phases into a communications revolution, what Alvin Toffler calls "the third wave." That information is power is more than a convenient slogan. More and more national economic development is determined by the control of information and its sale as a commodity on the international market. It is a great renewable resource that is controlled mainly by and for the West. Why? Because we have the technology, the organizations, the trained personnel—in short, the wherewithal to direct and manage information resources.

The Third World critics complain that this situation is a form of imperialism—the extension of power or authority or an advocacy of such extension—with the West brokering information, especially news as a commodity. "Once you sent armies—soldiers, ships and tanks;

now you send advertising agencies, television programs, movies, telex machines, and foreign correspondents," said one Third World critic.

A critical issue, as William Hachten has pointed out in *World News Prism* (Ames: Iowa State University Press, 1981), has to do with sender's rights vs. receiver's rights, with the right to inform vs. the right to be informed. This is the same argument we explored earlier (in terms of American constitutional law) with regard to the right of the speaker vs. the right of the listener. Is it right that the prevailing image in the world of most Third World nations is controlled by Western news agencies? Even if this coverage is largely that of earthquakes and coups, as Albert Hester of the University of Georgia has pointed out in research on Latin America?

The developing nations complain that they get a bad deal, that their countries are seen through Western eyes devoid of any understanding of local culture or history. The result for a country seeking foreign aid can, of course, be disastrous. If the prevailing image of that country is negative, if a country is perceived as a trivial, or worse yet, barbaric place with human rights violations or alarming customs, it may be punished by the denial of credit needed to develop economic projects. This discreditation has reputedly happened, much to the outrage of leaders in the developing world. They say that images of their countries are largely inaccurate and unrepresentative. It is as though the U.S. were depicted worldwide as a nation of snake worshipers because one obscure sect in Virginia does have this custom.

Of course, we Americans say that our freedom of the press demands that we tell it like it is, that we develop news stories (mainly for Western audiences) that will appeal to them. After all, foreign correspondents are not in their jobs to create representative educational materials, but to cover the things that we think are newsworthy. This difference of goals sets up a natural conflict.

Our view of freedom of the press is quite different from their's. Every year the Inter-American Press Association issues a report on Freedom of the Press in Latin America. That organization's definition centers on "absence of government controls." Any nation's press system that does not conform to this standard—essentially a Western article of faith—is deplored. Some commentators like John Nichols of Pennsylvania State University argue that this view "never has or will—or perhaps should—work in Latin America." The U.S. ideal of freedom of the press, he says, may not be transportable. It is a result of our own unique circumstance and constitutional development. A U.S. style "free press" may not be the best approach for the communications resources of Latin America. Our neighbors may need to use the media as tools in national development to teach people skills that will enhance business enterprises. This is not the function of Western style media.

Most persons involved in the cultural imperialism conflict agree that developing nations should create their own agencies and communications resources. Yet there is a strong vested interest for the major press associations—Associated Press, Reuters, Agence France-Presse, and United Press International—for such enterprises not to succeed.

In the late 1970s, I spoke with Alfred Oupobor in Lagos, Nigeria, during the time that he was engaged in setting up the Nigerian national news agency. "What," I asked him, "will your agency do that is different from AP?" "A great deal," he said. "Our interests and point of view are different. The capitals that are most important to us aren't the same ones where important Western news emanates." He planned to have correspondents stationed in cities that had special importance to Nigeria. "We want regular reports on the Organization for African Unity, from FAO in Rome, from the World Bank. We want news especially tailored to our needs." In addition, news would have a different ideological slant. It might conform with the Western objectivity model or move toward news values where the unusual, the bizarre gets top billing. Or it might follow a more partisan path and engage in government-sanctioned nation-building.

Some sympathetic Western observers have responded by saying that the U.S. should help the Third World by providing communication technology and training. But this "gift horse" also is fraught with problems. Both "gifts"—technology and training—demand commitments that would shape a country's communications environment and philosophy. We should remember that the Third World nations do not have communications media that evolved historically as ours did. The Third World media leaped from quite primitive printing to modern telecommunications systems in a single decade.

Students of information resources policy believe that every nation or region of the world should fashion its own system wherein local communications patterns—whether muffled drums, wall posters, or village gathering places—must be considered in the mix with modern technology. Frank Ugboajah, a Nigerian researcher, reports that in his country a traditional communicator, a "gong man", was more effective than radio for the transmission of certain messages. Not surprisingly,

Western technicians when installing Western equipment bring outside values and ideas about how training should be given. Whether it is cinema, radio, or television, the country is required to commit itself to using certain hardware and software that will determine what kind of system can be built and what kind of programming will be available, at least initially. Technology also tends to dictate the structure of the organization that will use it, and Western engineers tend to recommend Western structures and staffing patterns in countries that have their own way of doing things. As the British learned long ago, it is not possible for a British-style bureaucracy to function in some developing nations once the British civil servants left. That structure was based on a set of values, understandings, and working styles that evolved in Britain and other Commonwealth countries for the benefit and comfort of white Englishmen.

Coupled with the visible influence of technology is the more subtle effect of education and training. Again, Western nations have attempted to transplant American-style training programs to Asia, Latin America, and Africa with little regard for local nuances or conditions. In journalism education, for example, a model of professional training created originally to train newspaper reporters in the Middle West has been implemented without modification in distant places with different problems. While serving as an external examiner at a Nigerian University, I was surprised to learn that the students were great admirers of the *Washington Post's* Woodward and Bernstein because of their Watergate coverage. Some students advocated this kind of investigative journalism for West Africa. I learned that they were given encouragement for this approach in the classroom, but not always with the full understanding of how investigative reporting evolved in the U.S. and why. This was an instance where imported ideas were dangerous. At the time the country was under a military regime and vigorous reporting that probed the government could have been regarded as treason. As one Nigerian teacher told me, "These students don't understand that complete acceptance of American ideas about reporting could send them to the cooler." American educators have gone to developing nations with the best of intentions and have carried with them much that is useful; however, their efforts must be tempered to meet local needs.

Even the growing literature of international communications, produced mostly by Western scholars, is somewhat suspect in Third World nations. A considerable amount of research on mass media and international development assumed that Third World nations wanted to be like the West and that communications enterprises should follow a Western pattern. Only recently have international scholars, like Everett Rogers of Stanford University and Rita Atwood of the University of Texas, begun to reassess this "dominant paradigm" in development research.

When all is said and done, a Western presence in the Third World is a reality. Those nations are terribly dependent on Western resources, a condition linked to colonialism in the past. The British and French built transportation systems in many of these countries to extract natural resources. We have a presence in the Third World for defense, political, and economic reasons. Let's be frank about it. In the communications field, we want to sell our technology to the Third World; we would like to see their media emulate ours; we'd like to inculcate our philosophy and values to win their hearts and minds. Our purposes may be benevolent, but still we do have goals that serve our own national interests first and those of other nations, second. I agree with John Merrill that the Soviet Union and other Communist bloc nations try to exploit the charges of cultural and communications imperialism to their advantage. In their blunt, direct, and clumsy way, they want the same things we do. They are playing a "catch up" game because their communications technology is far behind ours.

Every nation should have its own communication policy. It should control its own destiny and not be stymied by the vested interests of Western companies and media organizations. What will result from such self-determination may not always please us, but importantly it will reflect the desires of the people of those nations to communicate with each other and with the rest of us in their own way. This is their right to freedom of expression, their right to communicate. The imposition of Western news values for many countries will be inappropriate. In some countries the media will evolve in the private sector, in others it will be a tool of government. That, as Walter Cronkite used to say, "is the way it is." And there is not much we can do about it. The policy that we in the U.S. fashion with regard to communications activity in the Third World is critical to our long-term relations with these nations. It is important that our response not be selfish for short-run gains. Our policy to date has been defensive, judgmental, and paternalistic. It needs modification and rethinking.

Barnet, Richard, and Ronald Muller. *Global Reach: The Power of the Multinational Corporation* (New York: Simon & Schuster, 1974).

Fenby, Jonathan. "The State of UNESCO: Background to the Information Debate," *Murrow Reports* (Medford, Mass: Tufts University, 1982).

Fisher, Glen. *American Communication in a Global Society* (Norwood, N.J.: Ablex, 1979).

Hachten, William. *World News Prism* (Ames: Iowa State University Press, 1981).

Hamelink, Cees J. *Cultural Autonomy in Global Communications* (New York: Longman, 1982).

Mankekar, D. R. *One-Way Flow: Neo-Colonialism via News Media* (New Delhi: Clarion Books, 1978).

_____. *Media and the Third World* (New Delhi: Indian Institute of Mass Communication, 1979).

Mattelart, Armand. *Mass Media, Ideologies, and the Revolutionary Movement* (Sussex, England: The Harvester Press, Ltd., 1980).

Merrill, J. C., et al. *Global Journalism* (New York: Longman, 1983).

Mueller, M. L. "Warnings of a Western Waterloo: The Influence of the International Organization of Journalists on the Evolution of the New International Information Order," *Murrow Reports,* Occasional Papers of the Edward R. Murrow Center of Public Diplomacy (Medford, Mass.: Tufts University, 1982).

Nordenstreng, Kaarle. *The Mass Media Declaration of UNESCO* (Norwood, N.J.: Ablex, 1982).

Nordenstreng, K., and Herbert Schiller, eds. *National Sovereignty and International Communication* (Norwood, N.J.: Ablex, 1979.

Revel, J. F. "Trouble with Latin America," translated by R. Kaplan, *Commentary,* Vol. 67, Fall 1979; pp. 47–50.

Richstad, Jim, and M. H. Anderson, eds. *Crisis in International News: Policies and Prospects* (New York: Columbia University Press, 1981).

Righter, Rosemary. *Whose News? Politics, Press and the Third World* (New York: Times Books, 1978).

Rogers, Everett. "Communication and Development: The Passing of the Dominant Paradigm." *Communication Research* (April 1976), 213 ff.

Schiller, H. I. *Communication and Cultural Domination* (New York: International Arts and Sciences Press, 1976).

Tunstall, Jeremy. *The Media Are American* (New York: Columbia University Press, 1977).

Ugboajah, Frank. *Communication Policies in Nigeria* (New York: UNESCO, 1981).

Index

Index

Berns, Walter, 11–12, 14
Bernstein, Carl, 90, 96, 187
Bickel, Alexander, 8
Bill of Rights, 3–4, 7, 32, 34, 38, 48–49, 52, 54
Birkhead, Douglas, 160
Black, Hugo Lafayette, 3–4, 8–9, 34
Blasi, Vince, 30
Blasphemy, 2
Blodgett, Cameron, 170–71
Bogart, John, 140
Boston Globe, 89, 99
Botein, Michael, 72
Bowman, William, 159
Boyer, John H., 42
Brandeis, Louis, 53
Branzburg v. *Hayes,* 34, 36
Brinkley, David, 105, 140
British Broadcasting Corporation, 22
British Press Council, 163
Broadcast ratings, 139
Brookings Institution report, 55
Brown, Charlene J., 14
Brucker, Herbert, 14, 84, 111
Buckley, William, 97
Buel, Ronald, 114, 116
Bukro, Casey, 166
Bulletin of ASNE, 19
Bureau of Labor Statistics, 151
Burger, Warren, 137
Burgoon, Judee and Michael, 101, 142, 148
 study, 91
Burke, Edmund, 12
Business coverage, 28

C

Cable, 65
 television, 55
 two-way, 57
Cable News Network, 66
Cahn, Edmond N., 3, 14
Campbell, Karlyn Kohrs, 84
Carey, James W., 153, 160
Cater, Douglass, 30

Central Intelligence Agency, 24
Center Magazine, The, 107
Chafee, Zechariah, 14
Chain ownership, 64
Chamberlain, Bill, 14
Chayefsky, Paddy, 169
Checkbook journalism, 121
Chicago Tribune, 164, 166
Chilling effect, 47
Christ, Jesus, 11
 Golden Rule of, 11
Cinemax, 66
Clarke, Peter, 77, 81
Cleveland Press, 62
Codes of ethics, 165–66
Cognitive effects, 78
Cohen, Stanley, 119
Cold War, 26
CBS, 23, 165
Commission on Freedom of the Press, 12, 14, 54, 139
Communication,
 defined, 179
 diversity, 61
 forms of, 12
 as a human right, 58
 imperialism, 175–76
 influence of, 176
 issuer of, 54
 theory, 158
Compaine, Benjamin, 63, 72
Comstock, George, 84
Confidential sources, 36
Confucian ethics, 11
Confucius, 11–12
Congress, defined, 4
Constitutional right of privacy, 53
Constraints on press freedom, 6
Consumer of communication, 54
Content, quality of, 68
Cooke, Janet, 157
Cooley, Thomas, 2–3, 14
Cooper, Kent, 39, 42
Copyright, 3, 6
Cranberg, Gilbert, 59
Cronkite, Walter, 188
Cross, Harold L., 33, 39, 42

Index

Index

Index

Index

Smith, Red, 90
Social construction of reality, 79
Social responsibility theory, 25, 40, 51, 171
Society of Professional Journalists, 149, 165
  code of ethics, 165
Soviet Union press, 49, 180–81
Southern Newspaper Publishers Association, 160
Spangler, Raymond, 42
Sports coverage, 29
Steffens, Lincoln, 90, 97
Stein, Robert, 85
Sterling, Christopher H., 72
Stevens, John P., 15
Stewart, Potter, 24, 35, 43
Stone, I. F., 29
Structure of media, 6
Subjective reporting, 106
Subjectivity, 105
Sullivan, Brian, 57
Sulzberger, Arthur, 165
Sunshine laws, 26, 31
  defined, 33
Supreme Court of the U.S., 3–4, 34, 47
Swedish Press Council, 163

T

Tarbell, Ida, 90, 96
TASS, 49, 180–81
Television, 93
  news, 92
  as a wasteland, 92
Theories of Mass Communication, 76
Third Wave, The, 184
Third World, The, 184
  journalistic systems, 181
  press, 178, 181, 183
Thomas, William, 165
Thomson newspaper, 64, 68
Thoreau, Henry David, 139–40, 148

Time, 43, 109
Time Inc., 66
Toffler, Alvin, 184

U

Ugboajah, Frank, 186, 190
UNESCO, 175–77, 179–80
United Press International, 66, 180, 186
United States Constitution, 3, 13, 21, 33, 38, 156
  structural provision of, 35
U.S. News & World Report, 109
United States Office of Education, 157
Unreasonable search and seizure, 3

V

Verifiable journalism, 108
Villard, Oswald Garrison, 63
Voltaire, 12

W

Wall Street Journal, 152
Warren, Samuel D., 53
Washington Post, 5, 23, 47, 111, 138, 157, 163, 187
Washington Star, 62, 68
Watchdog role, 17–19
Watergate, 24, 90
Watson, George, 169
Weaver, Paul H., 20, 30
Webster's Third New International Dictionary, 113, 155
Western communication imperialism, 175–91
Westmoreland, William, 23

200